Thank you to my wonderful friends for being constant sources of inspiration and light, and to my family for all they do. Extra special thanks to Lissie, Lucy and Leo for your words of wisdom, encouragement and humour.

MADELEINE

Thank you to my family and friends for helping me feel like I can achieve anything and thanks to Domy, my amazing dog who helped me through it all.

JISU

This paperback edition published in 2025 by Flying Eye Books.

First edition published in 2021 Flying Eye Books Ltd.
27 Westgate Street, London, E8 3RL.
www.flyingeyebooks.com

Represented by: Authorised Rep Compliance Ltd. Ground Floor,
71 Lower Baggot Street, Dublin, D02 P593, Ireland.
www.arccompliance.com

Edited by Emily Ball
Designed by Michelle Mac

13 5 7 9 10 8 6 4 2

UK ISBN: 978-1-83874-332-1

Printed in China on FSC® certified paper.

MADELEINE FINLAY

JISU CHOI

WEIRD AND WONDERFUL WAYS TO SAVE THE PLANET

FLYING EYE BOOKS

CONTENTS

HOW DOES THIS BOOK WORK?

From the breakfast table through to school, the park, the city and back home, each chapter of this book begins with a scene from all these familiar places and transforms them into futuristic versions of themselves. See what you can spot on each chapter opener, then turn the page to learn about the amazing technology each image showcases on the explainer spreads.

Then delve even deeper into these topics on the next spreads in the chapter. With plenty to explore and find on each spread, this book can be enjoyed all at once or chapter by chapter, depending on what mood you're in. There's a glossary at the back too, where all bold words are explained if you get stuck.

INTRODUCTION

Scientists can seem like very serious people. Some of them have lab coats, telescopes and microscopes, or beakers filled with mysterious chemicals. Others sit in stuffy offices looking at perplexing mathematical formulas or typing out complicated computer codes. But lots of them are busy doing peculiar experiments and thinking up weird and wonderful inventions. One challenge today's scientists are putting their minds to is the climate crisis. **Global warming** is causing some BIG problems for our planet, which is why scientists are finding imaginative new ways to help us protect the environment and improve our lifestyles.

In the not-so-distant future, these eco-friendly ideas might seem much more ordinary. Perhaps you'll use some of the green gadgets and gizmos included in this book! One day you could be turning kitchen waste into **energy**, producing power by stomping on the pavements while you walk to school and protecting the planet by wearing clothes made from old plastic bottles! So turn the page and take a look at what your life could be like in the years to come, and discover some of the amazing technology that could change our homes, cities and natural landscapes for the better.

06:30 TODAY'S MENU

9

BEETLES

SUN-DRIED OVEN

BEGIN RECIPE

7

6

3

BUGGY BONES

2

AT THE BREAKFAST TABLE

Whether it's using **algae** packaging or drinking cockroach milk, there are loads of weird and wonderful innovations out there that could make our day-to-day more sustainable for the planet. Starting from the moment we wake up in the morning and head to the kitchen for breakfast...

1. LOCUST LUNCH

Fancy crunching down on a cricket sandwich? The idea of eating bugs might make your skin crawl, but around two billion people worldwide are already enjoying insects in their lunches. With over 1,900 known edible species to pick from, many minibeasts are rich in protein, iron and calcium.

2. DOGGY DIET

Dogs are well-known for being unfussy eaters, so why not fill your furry friend's bowl with food made from maggots? **Larvae** of black soldier flies can be crushed and mixed with other ingredients like oats and potatoes to make nutritious pet food.

3. FUEL FROM FOOD

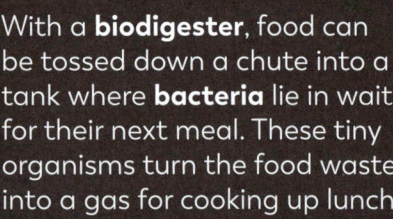

With a **biodigester**, food can be tossed down a chute into a tank where **bacteria** lie in wait for their next meal. These tiny organisms turn the food waste into a gas for cooking up lunch and also a mush that can be used as a fertiliser.

Over nine million tonnes of coffee beans are produced every year, brewed into the roughly two billion cups of coffee drunk every day!

FOOD WASTE

5. COFFEE POWER

A cup of coffee in the morning is a great way to power the day ahead. By extracting oil from used ground beans and turning it into fuel, coffee could help to power cars too. Old coffee can also be transformed into fire logs or even used as ink for printers.

4. KELP CARTONS

Imagine if, after finishing your juice, you didn't bin the packaging – but ate it! Cartons and capsules made from a kind of seaweed called kelp could one day be part of your breakfast. Seaweed packaging naturally degrades in the ground or dissolves with hot water, so it's much greener than plastic, even if you don't fancy eating it.

SUN-DRIED OVEN

7. SOLAR SUPPER

It may be far away, but the Sun is one of our most important natural resources here on Earth. Its power can even be used to cook food. A solar cooker works by collecting and focusing sunlight with lenses and reflective surfaces. The concentrated light hits the pot and heats up food Inside.

6. FATBERG FUEL

When cooking oil goes down the drain, it adds to a monstrous problem lurking below – fatbergs. Congealing with other non-flushable items like wet wipes, lumpy blockages can form and grow every time fat, oil and grease is poured into the pipes. Instead, these substances could be saved, collected and converted into fuel for vehicles.

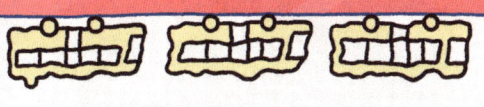

One monster fatberg discovered in London was a whopping 250m, which is longer than 20 double- decker buses.

INSERT COIN →

8. BEETLE JUICE

Unlike most insects, the Pacific beetle cockroach gives birth to live offspring. Before birth, whilst inside the mother, the baby cockroaches are fed with a pale-yellow liquid, which forms tiny crystals inside their guts. The liquid and crystals are both super nutritious. Rather than trying to milk cockroaches, scientists have suggested recreating the crystals in labs in order to make milk, bread and beer.

Scientists have estimated they would have to crush 1,000 cockroaches to get just 100g of the crystals.

9. SENSING A STINK

Futuristic packaging is being developed with sensors that monitor the **fungi**, **bacteria** or gases produced by food as it goes bad. When the sensors detect stuff getting stinky, they transmit a warning signal to a nearby device. Your phone could suggest recipes to use up food that might turn bad, so you don't end up throwing it away. Anyone for a strawberry yoghurt and stilton sandwich?

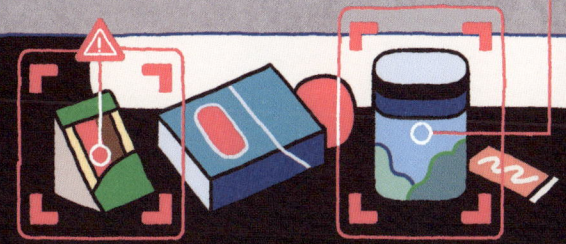

BEETLES FOR BREAKFAST

Have you ever wondered what food we might be eating in the future?
Pills that give you all the nutrition you could ever need, or even
3D-printed pizza... Our meals might change all the time but
finding new kinds of food could really help the planet.

WHAT'S THE PROBLEM?

From delicious burgers to sizzling steaks, cows are eaten
across the world but they also have a *moo-sive* impact
on Earth. Cows' burps and farts produce **methane**, a
gas that goes into the **atmosphere** and traps heat from
the Sun. One cow wouldn't make much difference, but
there are roughly 1.5 billion of them on the planet.
Millions of other animals, such as sheep, pigs and
chickens, are also reared for food. Like all living things,
they need to drink, eat and have space to move
around – using up lots of water, resources and land.
Millions of trees are cut down every year to make room
for raising livestock, which sends **carbon dioxide** into
the atmosphere and destroys habitats for wild animals.

Eating beef once a
day for a year would
produce the same amount
of greenhouse gases
(like **carbon dioxide**)
as driving a car from
Paris to Shanghai.

Scientists are always thinking of new ways to reduce the impact of our food. They've even considered putting cows on seaweed diets to cut down their **methane** output, or collecting their burps for fuel.

One cow can produce up to 200kg of methane a year.

INSECT FARMS

There is one idea which could be much more straightforward than trying to reduce the impact of farm animals. We could eat something smaller, which uses less land and fewer resources. Something like ... insects.

Insects are full of vitamins and minerals and are a great meat alternative. Caterpillars, locusts and fly **larvae** all contain elements such as zinc, which boosts the immune system, and iron, which carries **oxygen** around your body. Critters can be crushed or cooked to make them more appetising. Flour made from mealworms could be used to bake a cake, or the protein from beetles might one day be mixed into fake bacon for a nutritious bee-L-T.

Creepy-crawlies can also eat waste and plants thatpeople and livestock can't consume. We can even farm insects in cities and urban environments to save space.

Some red food colouring found in products like cake or juice is made from crushed bugs called cochineal.

MODERN MEAT

If you don't fancy munching on mealworms, never fear. Here are some more environmentally friendly food alternatives...

FAKE STEAKS

Scientists are working out how to grow meat in laboratories. First, a sample of cells needs to be taken from an animal's muscle tissue. This is called a **biopsy**. With some clever chemistry, the cells can be multiplied to create synthetic meat, which can then be turned into things like chicken wings or sausages. The first lab grown steak has actually already been served, but something like this still takes enormous amounts of **energy** (and money) to make. With other more energy efficient meat alternatives around, it might be a while until a test tube takeaway is on the menu.

The first ever lab-grown burger took over two years and cost £215,000 to make!

MUSHROOM MEAT

Tiny, spider-web-like tendrils from **fungi** can also be turned into cheat meat. When you think about fungi, you probably conjure up images of mushrooms sprouting from the ground. But down in the soil below, under the mushroom's cap, is a mass of sprawling white threads. Similar to roots, these are called **mycelium**. To build mock-burgers and bacon, mycelium is fermented, heated and then mushed up with flavourings so it mimics meaty textures.

FISH-FREE FOOD

As they journey from ocean to plate, fish can create a big **carbon footprint**. Fishing can also harm seabeds and coral reefs, and whales, dolphins and sharks often get stuck in the nets. Scientists are working on alternatives using something called 'heme', an iron-rich molecule found in plants and animals. In humans, heme in our blood helps to carry **oxygen** from the lungs to the rest of our body. It also gives blood its red colour, and meat its characteristic texture and flavour! Handily, it can be cultivated from yeast to create a delicious fake-fish dish.

A single teaspoon of soil can hold up to a billion **bacteria**!

SOIL SOUP

A bowl of **bacterial** soup might just be the futuristic food scientists have been searching for. Chemists have created a powdery protein made from soil bacteria, **carbon dioxide** (CO_2), water and electricity. Applying electricity to the water produces bubbles of **hydrogen**, which together with CO_2 extracted from the **atmosphere**, feed the bacteria. This mixture then ferments, a bit like vinegar, and the yellow frothy soup it produces is fed on to hot rollers to dry out – turning it into a powder similar to flour. It's said not to taste like anything at all, which means it would be a perfect addition to foods to make them more nutritious, at very little cost to the planet.

IN THE BATHROOM

Getting clean has never been so green...
Futuristic bathrooms could use space technology
to recycle water, smart mirrors to check your health
and special loos to turn your poo into power!

25°C

07:30 ALARM

Don't forget your vitamins!

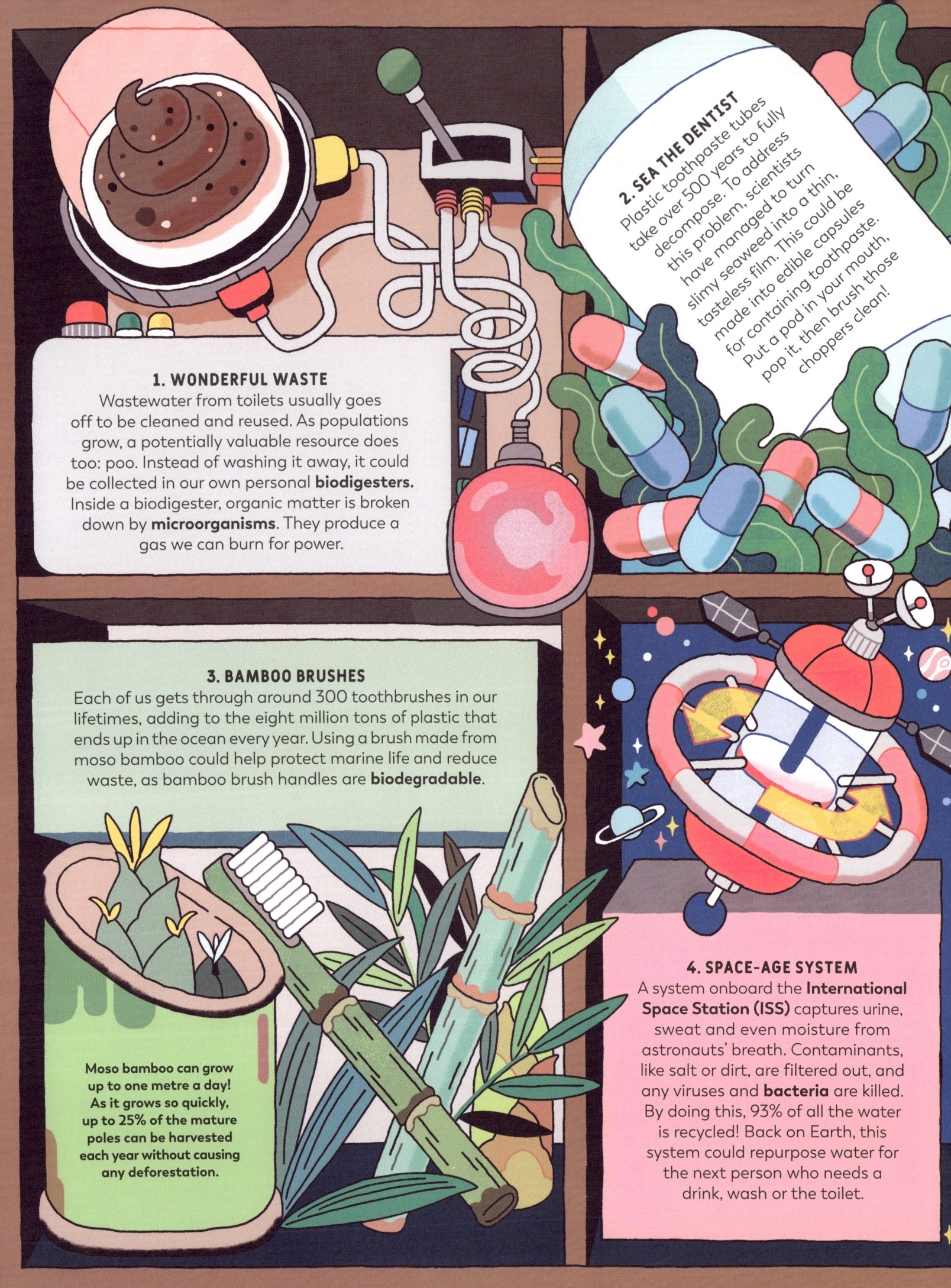

1. WONDERFUL WASTE

Wastewater from toilets usually goes off to be cleaned and reused. As populations grow, a potentially valuable resource does too: poo. Instead of washing it away, it could be collected in our own personal **biodigesters**. Inside a biodigester, organic matter is broken down by **microorganisms**. They produce a gas we can burn for power.

2. SEA THE DENTIST

Plastic toothpaste tubes take over 500 years to fully decompose. To address this problem, scientists have managed to turn slimy seaweed into a thin, tasteless film. This could be made into edible capsules for containing toothpaste. Put a pod in your mouth, pop it, then brush those choppers clean!

3. BAMBOO BRUSHES

Each of us gets through around 300 toothbrushes in our lifetimes, adding to the eight million tons of plastic that ends up in the ocean every year. Using a brush made from moso bamboo could help protect marine life and reduce waste, as bamboo brush handles are **biodegradable**.

Moso bamboo can grow up to one metre a day! As it grows so quickly, up to 25% of the mature poles can be harvested each year without causing any deforestation.

4. SPACE-AGE SYSTEM

A system onboard the **International Space Station (ISS)** captures urine, sweat and even moisture from astronauts' breath. Contaminants, like salt or dirt, are filtered out, and any viruses and **bacteria** are killed. By doing this, 93% of all the water is recycled! Back on Earth, this system could repurpose water for the next person who needs a drink, wash or the toilet.

5. MOSS MAT

A mat made of moss gives you the feeling of grass between your toes, and soaks up steam and water that comes out when you leave the shower. Moss is a type of plant called a 'bryophyte', which means it doesn't produce flowers, seeds or roots, and prefers a moist habitat – like your bathroom.

In the First World War, moss was used to mop up blood from nasty wounds. It is super absorbent and has antiseptic properties, keeping injuries clean and dry.

6. MIRROR MAGIC

Mirror, mirror on the wall, who's the healthiest of them all? Equipped with sensors, these smart mirrors could scan your eyes, skin and breath and gather all sorts of data from them. This data would then be fed into a computer for an **algorithm** to analyse and check for symptoms of illness.

7. SEE-THROUGH SOLAR

Solar-power windows catch **energy** from the Sun and convert it into electricity. The Sun radiates energy in different **wavelengths**. We can see some wavelengths in the form of visible light, but not all. The windows trap invisible **ultraviolet (UV)** and **infrared** wavelengths but let visible light through, so the bathroom is bright and there's extra electricity to power your hairdryer!

8. BIO BEADS

Microbeads are tiny plastic beads, smaller than a grain of sand, found in many bathroom products, like toothpaste and shower gels. These beads get washed into rivers and oceans, where they are accidentally eaten by aquatic animals. Luckily, scientists are creating a new eco-bead alternative. Made from cellulose (the stuff plants use to stay firm and upright), these beads are **biodegradable** and safe to send down the sink!

9. MEDICAL MUCUS

Instead of plasters that fall off your knees, one day you could be sealing wounds with glue inspired by slugs. When it's threatened, the Dusky Arion slug excretes a sticky mucus, which attaches the slug to the surface it's on. This prevents it from being grabbed by predators like birds. Scientists have designed a medical glue based on the mucus for patching people up during surgery.

FEELING POWERFUL

Power fuels our lives. From boiling the kettle in the morning to setting your morning alarm, we use power day and night. All this **energy** has to come from somewhere and our current fuel sources put a strain on the environment. Luckily for us, there are plenty of innovative ideas that can reclaim power after it's been washed down the drain...

WHAT'S THE PROBLEM?

The power we use comes from lots of places, but globally we get most of it from oil, coal and gas. These are known as **fossil fuels** and are formed by decomposing plants and animals that have been buried underground for millions of years. To release the **energy** stored inside fossil fuels, we dig them up and burn them, liberating a whole bunch of **carbon dioxide** at the same time. This contributes to **global warming** and pollutes our air, which is why the hunt is on for clean, green and futuristic ways to power our lives.

POO POWER

All over the world waste is collected from toilets, farms and even pets to provide power! For starters, poo can be used to heat our homes. In the sewers below cities, our waste can reach a balmy 15–20 degrees Celsius. Rather than letting the warmth go unused, **heat pumps** can draw it out and send it back to nearby buildings.

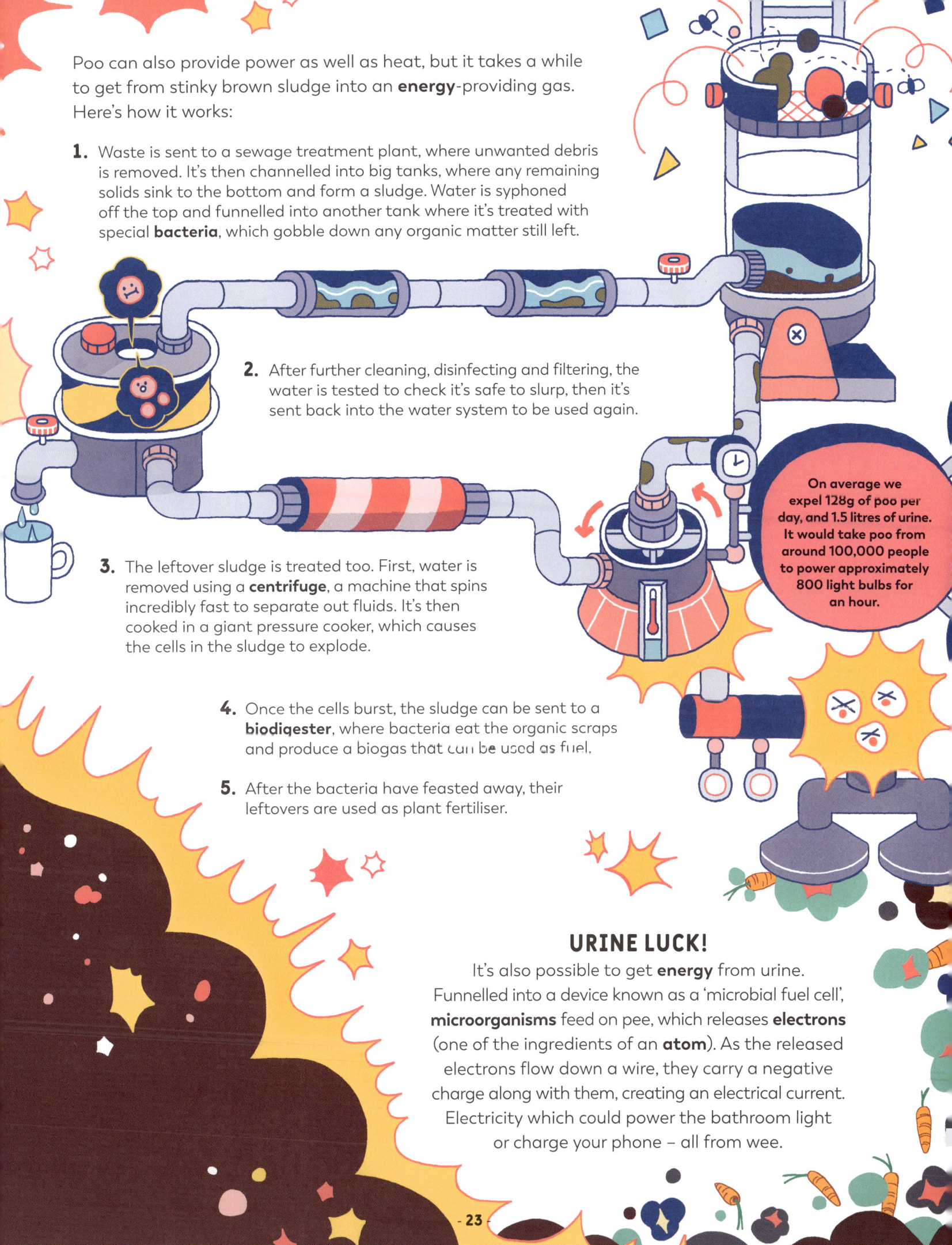

Poo can also provide power as well as heat, but it takes a while to get from stinky brown sludge into an **energy**-providing gas. Here's how it works:

1. Waste is sent to a sewage treatment plant, where unwanted debris is removed. It's then channelled into big tanks, where any remaining solids sink to the bottom and form a sludge. Water is syphoned off the top and funnelled into another tank where it's treated with special **bacteria**, which gobble down any organic matter still left.

2. After further cleaning, disinfecting and filtering, the water is tested to check it's safe to slurp, then it's sent back into the water system to be used again.

3. The leftover sludge is treated too. First, water is removed using a **centrifuge**, a machine that spins incredibly fast to separate out fluids. It's then cooked in a giant pressure cooker, which causes the cells in the sludge to explode.

4. Once the cells burst, the sludge can be sent to a **biodigester**, where bacteria eat the organic scraps and produce a biogas that can be used as fuel.

5. After the bacteria have feasted away, their leftovers are used as plant fertiliser.

On average we expel 128g of poo per day, and 1.5 litres of urine. It would take poo from around 100,000 people to power approximately 800 light bulbs for an hour.

URINE LUCK!

It's also possible to get **energy** from urine. Funnelled into a device known as a 'microbial fuel cell', **microorganisms** feed on pee, which releases **electrons** (one of the ingredients of an **atom**). As the released electrons flow down a wire, they carry a negative charge along with them, creating an electrical current. Electricity which could power the bathroom light or charge your phone – all from wee.

WONDERFUL WATER

If all this toilet tech is making your stomach churn, never fear.
There's something else found in the bathroom that can produce
a whole lot of power too ... and it's a lot less stinky!

MAKING WAVES

Have you ever been hit by an ocean wave while swimming?
Then you'll know how strong water can be. That's why scientists have
designed lots of different wave-powered systems to collect **energy**.
One idea is to build a carpet on the seabed from rubber mats that
move up and down as waves pass. The movement pushes pumps
attached to the mats in and out – absorbing some of the energy
from the waves and turning it into electricity.

The scientists who designed
the sea carpet were inspired by
muddy ocean floors that slow
down waves passing overhead.
They noticed fishermen in the
Gulf of Mexico took their boats
to particularly muddy areas
when a storm arrived, as the
waves weren't as strong.

KELP ME!

Kelp, a type of seaweed **algae**,
could also help us produce power.
Like plants, algae can turn sunlight
into food. This is called 'photosynthesis',
a chemical reaction that uses the Sun's
rays to transform **carbon dioxide**
and water into sugar and **oxygen**.
During photosynthesis, algae also
produce electrons which can be
harnessed to generate electricity.

Some types of kelp can
grow 50cm in a single day,
getting up to 50m in length.
If you grew 50cm every day
for a year, you'd end up almost
twice the height of London's
Big Ben clock tower.

WATER YOU THINKING?

Have you ever heard of water referred to as H_2O? This describes what water is made from – **hydrogen** (H) and **oxygen** (O), bound together. These two elements are pretty important. Hydrogen is the most abundant element in the universe, and the oxygen we breathe in keeps us alive. Engineers have designed devices known as 'hydrogen fuel cells' that take hydrogen and oxygen and mix them together to create electricity and water. As the devices produce water rather than pollution, hydrogen fuel cells are a promising power source for cars and buses. The only problem is, although there's lots of hydrogen elsewhere in space, there isn't actually much of it back here on Earth – which usually means making it ourselves from **fossil fuels**.

FLYING HIGH

Scientists have tested a method for turning seawater into jet fuel. Surprisingly, ocean water has a higher concentration of **carbon dioxide** than air. The scientists who spotted this used it to their advantage by splitting water into **hydrogen**, **oxygen** and carbon dioxide with the power of electricity. Then, they recombined the hydrogen and carbon dioxide to create fuel. As the process currently takes up a lot of **energy**, here on land we won't be using it any time soon but one day it could be a great source of power for ships out at sea.

IN THE CITY

Cities can be polluted places, but with some cutting-edge technology we could clean them up and create green spaces to live, travel and work in. Filled to the brim with bicycles and scooters, super-quick solar trains running on stilts, plant-skyscrapers and plenty of areas to walk, the cities of the future are already becoming a reality.

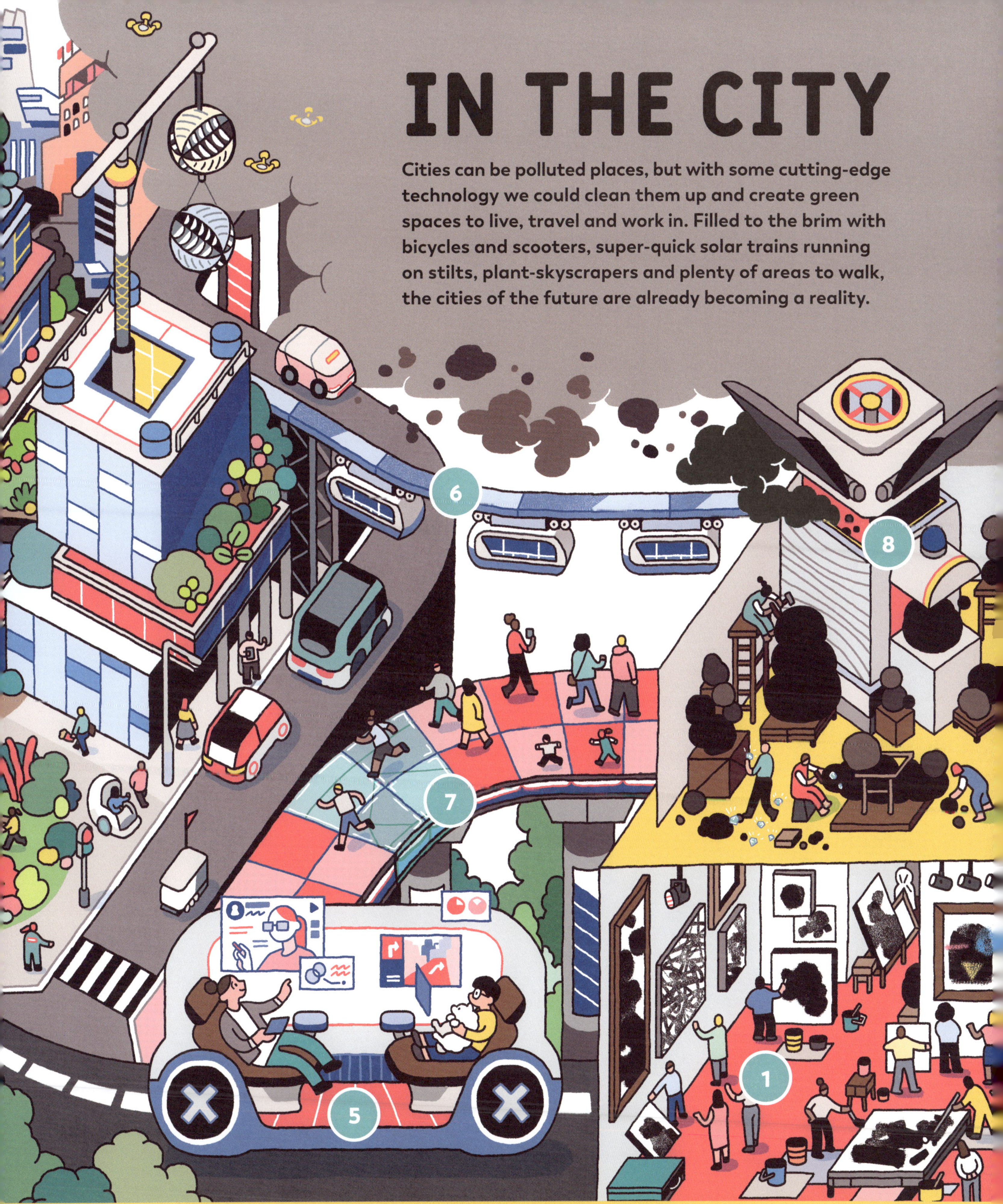

6 SKY-HIGH COMMUTE

7 PLASTIC PATHS

8 SOOT SUCKS

9 FOOT POWER

10 GOING UNDERGROUND

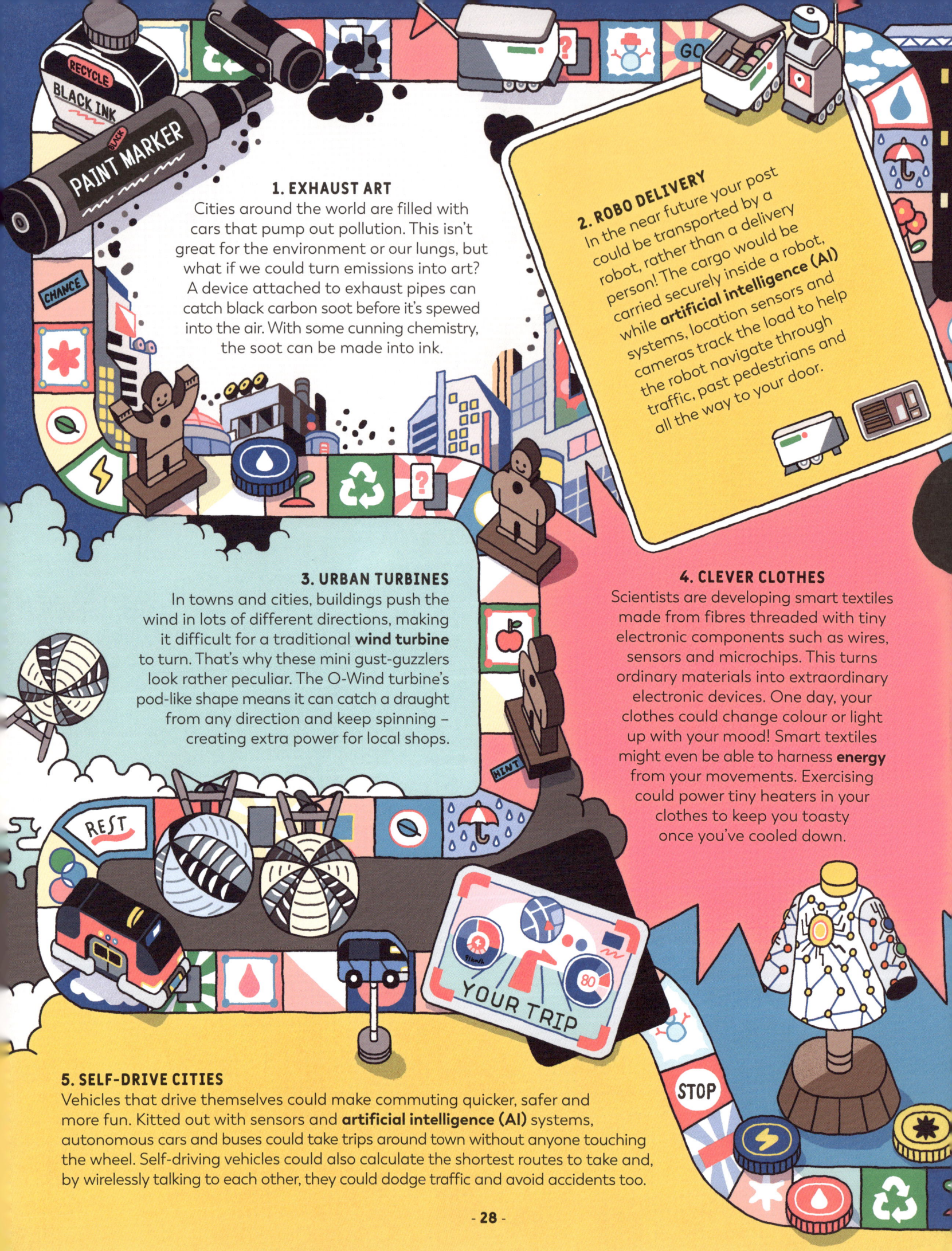

1. EXHAUST ART

Cities around the world are filled with cars that pump out pollution. This isn't great for the environment or our lungs, but what if we could turn emissions into art? A device attached to exhaust pipes can catch black carbon soot before it's spewed into the air. With some cunning chemistry, the soot can be made into ink.

2. ROBO DELIVERY

In the near future your post could be transported by a robot, rather than a delivery person! The cargo would be carried securely inside a robot, while **artificial intelligence (AI)** systems, location sensors and cameras track the load to help the robot navigate through traffic, past pedestrians and all the way to your door.

3. URBAN TURBINES

In towns and cities, buildings push the wind in lots of different directions, making it difficult for a traditional **wind turbine** to turn. That's why these mini gust-guzzlers look rather peculiar. The O-Wind turbine's pod-like shape means it can catch a draught from any direction and keep spinning – creating extra power for local shops.

4. CLEVER CLOTHES

Scientists are developing smart textiles made from fibres threaded with tiny electronic components such as wires, sensors and microchips. This turns ordinary materials into extraordinary electronic devices. One day, your clothes could change colour or light up with your mood! Smart textiles might even be able to harness **energy** from your movements. Exercising could power tiny heaters in your clothes to keep you toasty once you've cooled down.

5. SELF-DRIVE CITIES

Vehicles that drive themselves could make commuting quicker, safer and more fun. Kitted out with sensors and **artificial intelligence (AI)** systems, autonomous cars and buses could take trips around town without anyone touching the wheel. Self-driving vehicles could also calculate the shortest routes to take and, by wirelessly talking to each other, they could dodge traffic and avoid accidents too.

6. SKY-HIGH COMMUTE

To make the most of the available space in crushed cities, traffic could be stuck on stilts. Above our heads, caterpillar-like pods hanging from metal arches could whizz people from here to there without disturbing anyone on the ground. They could even be partly powered by **solar panels**, catching light from the Sun and providing shade for the people below.

7. PLASTIC PATHS

Engineers have worked out how to turn plastic rubbish into small pellets that can be mixed with other materials to make a substance for resurfacing roads or building pavements. Plastic has already been used in roads all around the world; Zwolle, a city in the Netherlands, even has a 30-metre cycle path made of recycled bottles and packaging.

The recycled plastic in Zwolle's cycle path is equivalent to 218,000 plastic cups!

8. SOOT SUCKS

Imagine a huge tower that acts like a vacuum cleaner for pollution. It sucks in dirty air called **smog** and filters it, separating clean air from the sooty particles. The resulting powder includes carbon, which when squashed, transforms into sparkling diamonds. So with a big vacuum and some alchemy, you can make gems out of dirt!

9. FOOT POWER

Wouldn't it be great if the ground harvested **energy** from every step you took? Floors made from **piezoelectric materials** can transform pressure from pounding feet into electricity. In stadiums and train stations, our stomps and strides could be a fantastic source of power.

10. GOING UNDERGROUND

Hidden away from the hustle and bustle, underground buildings could give us more space and protect us from the elements above – like super-hot summers and blowing gales. Designed to ensure enough light and fresh air is channelled in, subterranean dwellings would mean lots more of us could live in cities whilst keeping them filled with trees, birds and bees.

STOP

REST

RECYCLE

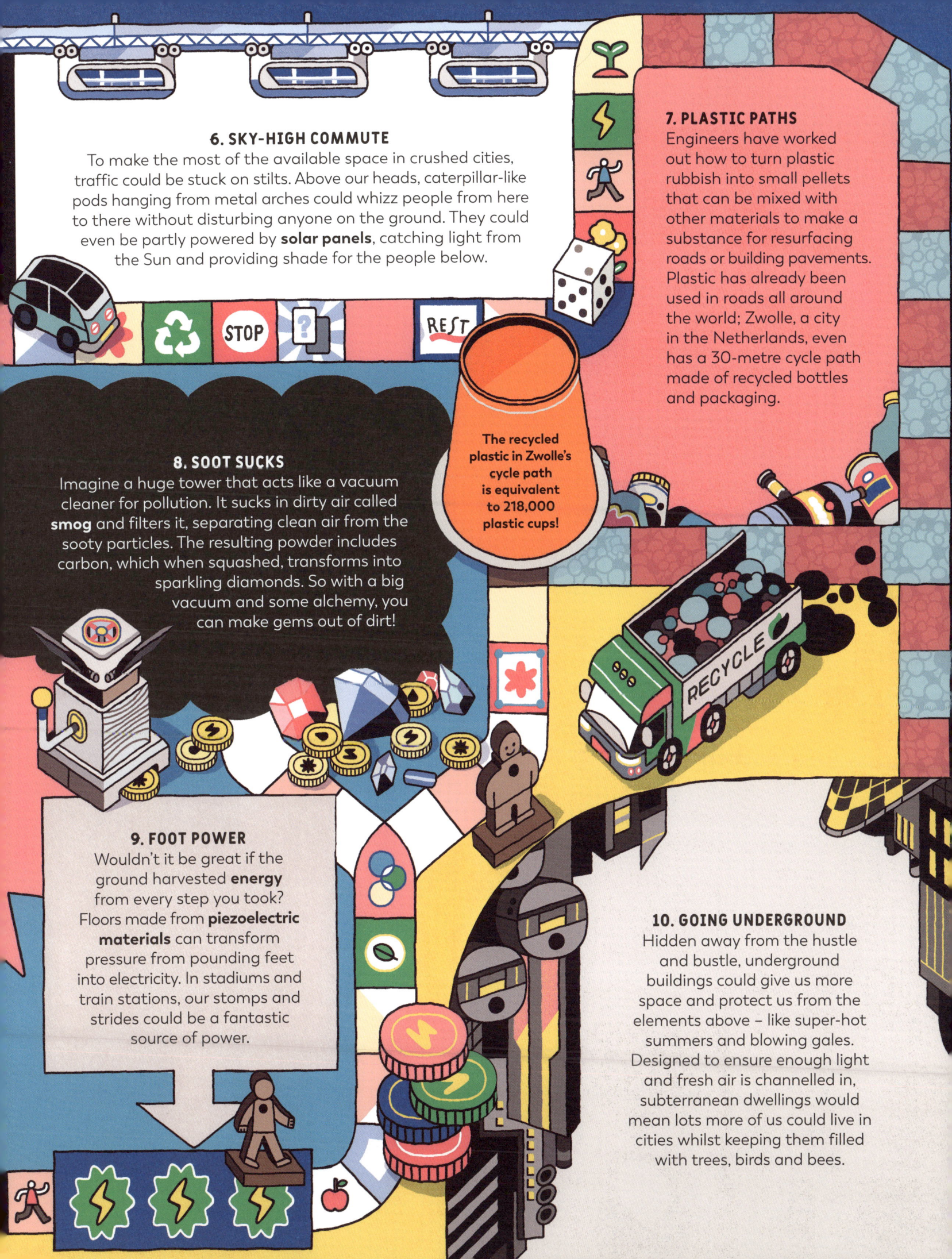

MOVING FORWARD

Our travel habits have a big impact on the planet, so to keep moving, we need to find cleaner, greener transport. The first step will be coming up with solutions for getting around, but with cities always struggling for spare room, these new ideas will need to be space efficient too.

WHAT'S THE PROBLEM?

Cars, buses and vans are great for getting from A to B but it's what comes out of these contraptions that's the problem. Unwanted gases and smoke particles escape from exhaust pipes and drift up into the air around us. When we breathe in these emissions, they get into our lungs, hearts and even our brains. This makes **air pollution** bad for the health of humans, as well as animals and the environment. In cities, where there are lots of vehicles driving around, pollution is particularly problematic.

We can't magically take automobiles off the roads. How would everyone get to where they need to go? But we can think of some greener alternatives. New ways of travelling could reduce the number of fuel-burning cars and buses – meaning less dirty air and more space for bicycles, pedestrians and parks!

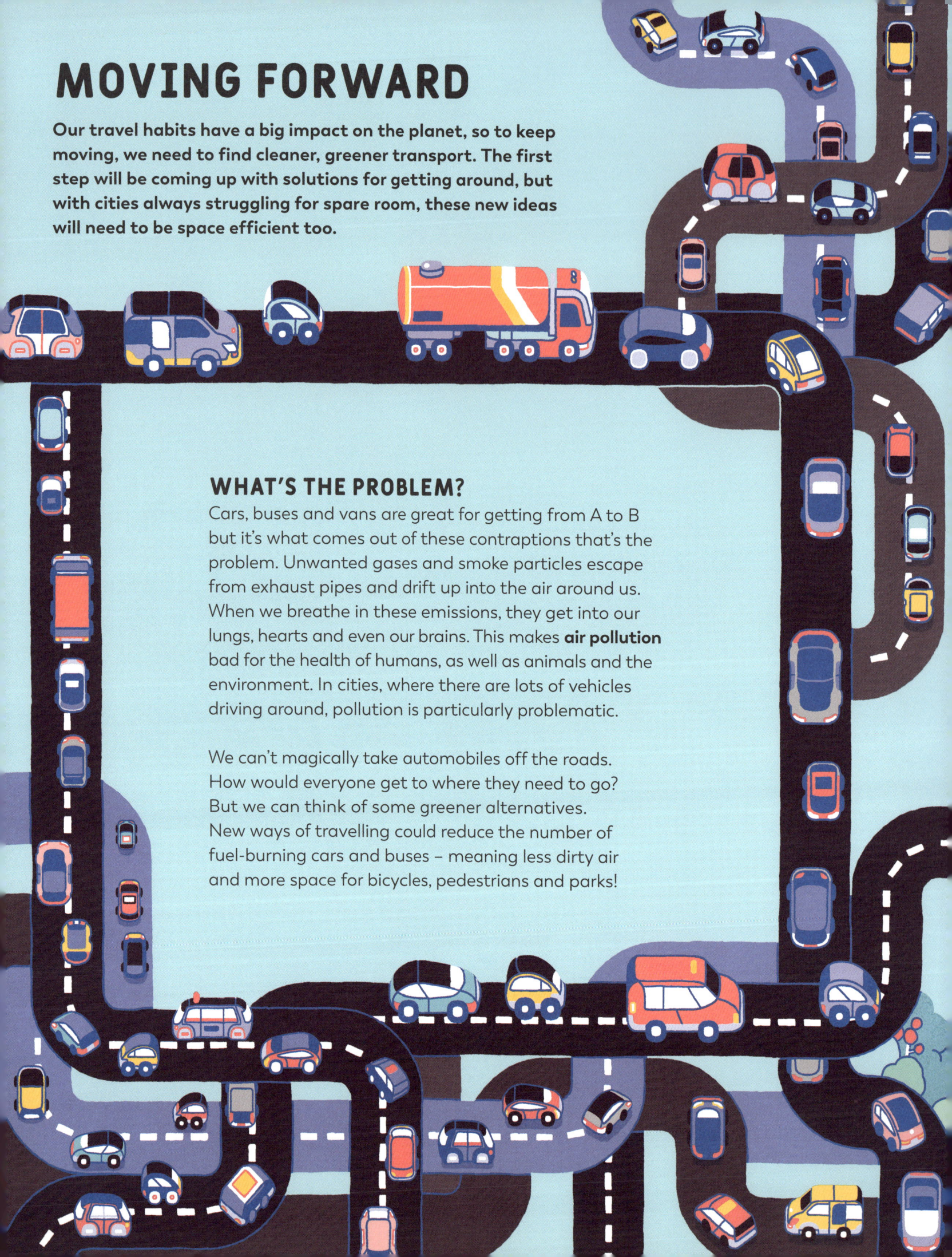

HIGH IN THE SKY

In the future, we could be zipping through the air in electric flying taxis! A bit like helicopters, urban aerial vehicles would have a pod for carrying people or cargo and spinning blades to lift them into the sky. By making use of all that room above our heads, these taxis could help to reduce traffic – and would be great for a bit of sightseeing.

Scientists are keen to make these flying pods environmentally friendly, meaning they would need to run on some seriously powerful batteries. For now, scientists have yet to create a battery efficient or light enough to really get the idea off the ground, but engineers are getting closer to finding a solution. In the meantime, back on solid ground there are some other great travel alternatives in the making.

WHEELIE COOL

In the middle of a South Korean highway is a cycle path almost 50km long. **Solar panels** above the path shelter cyclists from the Sun and generate electricity. This can be used to power the highway's night lights and provide charging points for **electric cars**. Building solar cycle paths between towns and cities would help commuters get their daily exercise, whilst generating **energy**, and all without emitting any pollution!

It's not just South Korea with futuristic cycle lanes. One Polish city has built a glow-in-the-dark path. Particles in the surface called 'luminophores' absorb sunlight during the day, gleaming blue when it gets dark and illuminating the way for night-time cyclists. And to get away from busy roads, residents of Xiamen, a city in China, can glide along a purpose-built cycle 'skyway', five metres above the ground.

TRAVEL PLANS

Space-saving cycle lanes and flying taxis are great for inter-city travel, but what about long distance journeys? Aeroplanes are incredible, taking people thousands of kilometres in just a few hours, but they emit a lot of pollution. That's why scientists are dreaming up different ways of travelling around the globe.

MAGNIFICENT MAGNETS

Maglev trains are named after their technology – magnetic levitation. Powerful magnets on the tracks and undercarriage of the train repel each other, pushing the train upwards so that it floats off the ground. Magnets along the sides of the track guide and propel the train forwards. By hovering on a cushion of air, Maglev trains avoid friction from the track, allowing them to travel hundreds of kilometres per hour.

Japan's high-speed trains can reach 320kmph. To reduce air resistance, engineers were inspired by the sleek shape of a kingfisher's bill, which allows it to dive seamlessly into water. Mimicking this helped the trains to run faster and quieter.

Every year there is a competition to design and build pods for a hyperloop system. Winners have managed to get their pods to travel more than 450kmph down a prototype tube.

GOING LOOPY

Even maglev trains are snail-paced next to the potential of hyperloops... Imagine whizzing from London to Berlin in less time than it takes to bake a cake. You'd have to be moving at over 1,000 kilometres per hour! That's the plan for hyperloops. Pods that levitate using powerful magnets could be flung through super-long tubes. Most of the air would need to be hoovered out of the tubes to create an almost frictionless chute to glide down, like sucking juice through a straw!

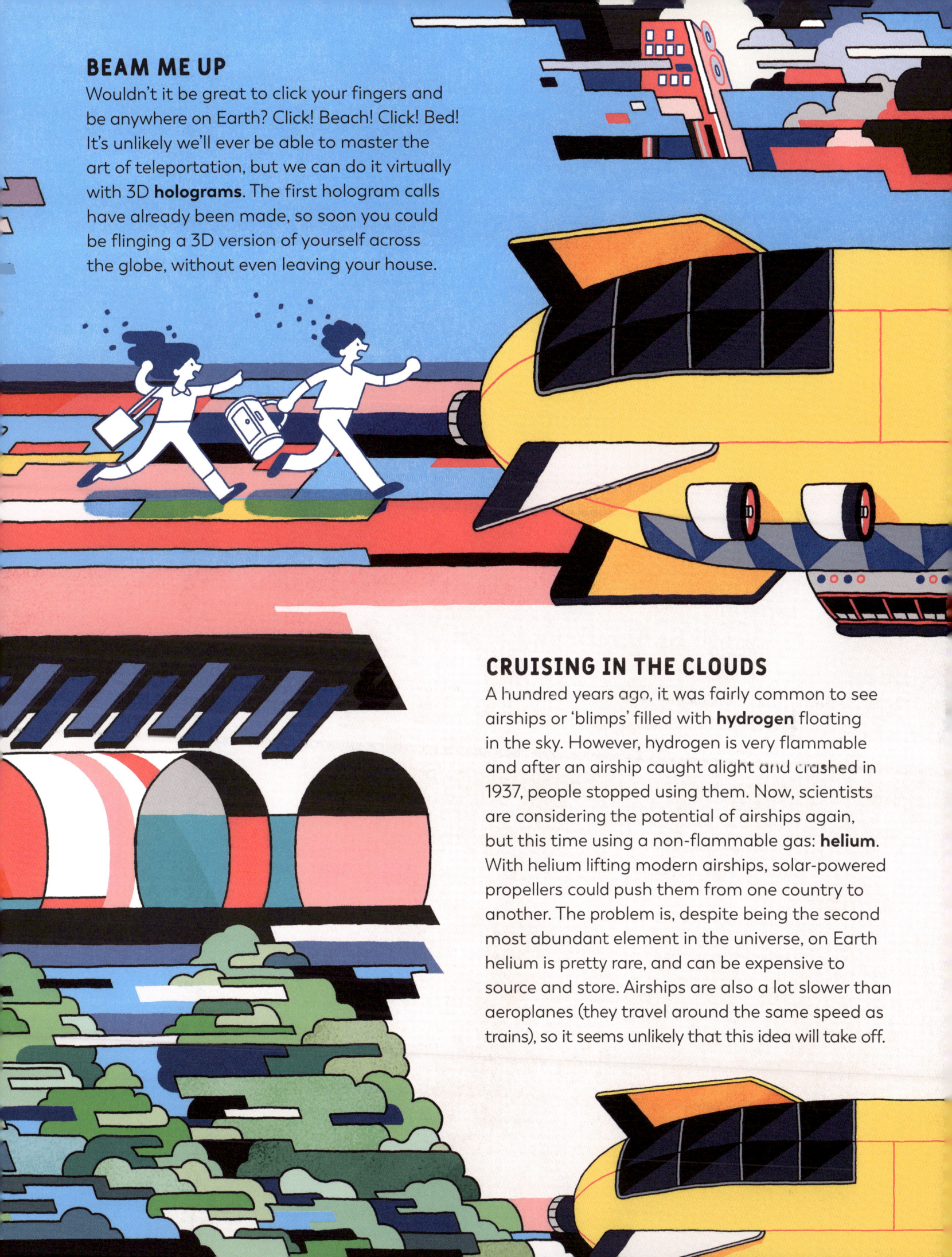

BEAM ME UP

Wouldn't it be great to click your fingers and be anywhere on Earth? Click! Beach! Click! Bed! It's unlikely we'll ever be able to master the art of teleportation, but we can do it virtually with 3D **holograms**. The first hologram calls have already been made, so soon you could be flinging a 3D version of yourself across the globe, without even leaving your house.

CRUISING IN THE CLOUDS

A hundred years ago, it was fairly common to see airships or 'blimps' filled with **hydrogen** floating in the sky. However, hydrogen is very flammable and after an airship caught alight and crashed in 1937, people stopped using them. Now, scientists are considering the potential of airships again, but this time using a non-flammable gas: **helium**. With helium lifting modern airships, solar-powered propellers could push them from one country to another. The problem is, despite being the second most abundant element in the universe, on Earth helium is pretty rare, and can be expensive to source and store. Airships are also a lot slower than aeroplanes (they travel around the same speed as trains), so it seems unlikely that this idea will take off.

AT SCHOOL

There's a lot we can discover at school – like how to tackle tricky maths equations and wire a circuit powered by **solar panels**. The way we learn evolves all the time. We've gone from scribbling down sums with chalk and slate to watching online video lessons at home. Technology can give us new and improved ways to learn, as well as helping us adapt to a changing world.

1. TEXT A TEACHER

Have you ever noticed that adults often don't know the answers to the most interesting questions? This can be annoying when you're stuck on a homework problem. That's why scientists are developing virtual teachers: robots that use **artificial intelligence** to automatically answer student queries. In the future, when you're learning remotely, you could text a robo-tutor for help!

2. GROWING GARMENTS

Isn't it annoying when you grow out of your new school trousers in just a few months? Origami-inspired clothes could help avoid these growing pains, as well as endless shopping trips. Materials known as 'auxetics' have special kinds of pleats, so they can expand longer and wider. This means garments can grow with the wearer.

1 YEAR **2 YEARS** **3 YEARS** **4 YEARS** **5 YEARS**

3. LANGUAGE ON DEMAND

Hello! Ciao! Merhaba! Communicating with people from around the world means we can share ideas and news. In the future, handy headphones could take on the role of translator for us. When you chat to someone who speaks another language, a microphone in the headphones listens to what they're saying and a clever computer switches it into the language you understand.

Mandarin Chinese is the world's most popular native language. Almost one billion people speak it as their first language!

你早，你们好吗？

GOOD MORNING, HOW ARE YOU?

4. CEMETERY SCIENCE

When a loved one dies, this can be a sad and painful time. But what if something good could come of something sad? Around 150,000 people die every day and a lot of the bodies are sent to crematoriums. These crematoriums produce hot gas – which could be piped to buildings such as schools to heat them up. It might sound scary, but it's a clever way to reuse **energy** that would otherwise go to waste.

RIP

5. POWER OF THE CROWD

Get your classmates involved in a 'citizen science' project! You'll find loads of activities online, from tagging penguins in photos (to count them, not for their social media) to listening out for manatee calls. In the real world you can count butterflies or record slug-sightings. Researchers study this data, provided by people around the world, to learn about animals and the environment.

6. LIVING WALLS

A wall covered in plants could be the perfect place for a hands-on science experiment. You and your friends could see how roots grow, flowers blossom and how these habitats provide homes to all kinds of insects. Living walls also help to keep buildings cool in the summer and warm in the winter. Research shows that being around greenery makes humans happier too!

7. SOLAR SCHOOLS

In classrooms that get lots of sun, desks could turn light into electricity – just plug in to power your mobile phone (that's if the teacher hasn't already confiscated it). Mini **solar panels** could also be built into bike helmets, backpacks and portable speakers – so you can play your favourite tunes on the way home from school using the power of the Sun.

Every hour around 600 quintillion (600, 000, 000, 000, 000, 000, 000) joules of energy from the Sun reach the Earth. That's more than the amount of energy humans use in a year!

8. VIRTUAL LESSONS

Augmented reality could let you do dissections without hurting any frogs, or watch a dinosaur stampede without travelling back in time. Augmented reality works by placing objects, people, animals or information into the image you see on your device when using the camera – making it seem as if they're in the room, but you're looking at your screen!

9. COOLING KITS

These futuristic PE kits have **bacteria** inside (and not because they haven't been washed in a while). They're designed so that when you start sweating, the bacteria swell, opening the flaps for a refreshing breeze. Once the sweat has dried, the bacteria shrink and the flaps close. This could help you stay at the perfect temperature during a game of football.

10. SUBWAY SOLUTION

Underground trains can be sweltering. Rather than letting all that heat go to waste, hot air escaping out of ventilation shafts can be harnessed to warm up water. This could be sent to nearby buildings, like schools and homes, to get them nice and toasty. If you got the train to school, you'd be helping to warm up your classroom before you even arrived!

Most of the heat underground is produced by trains as they accelerate, brake and travel through tunnels. New York's Subway system can reach a sweltering 41°C.

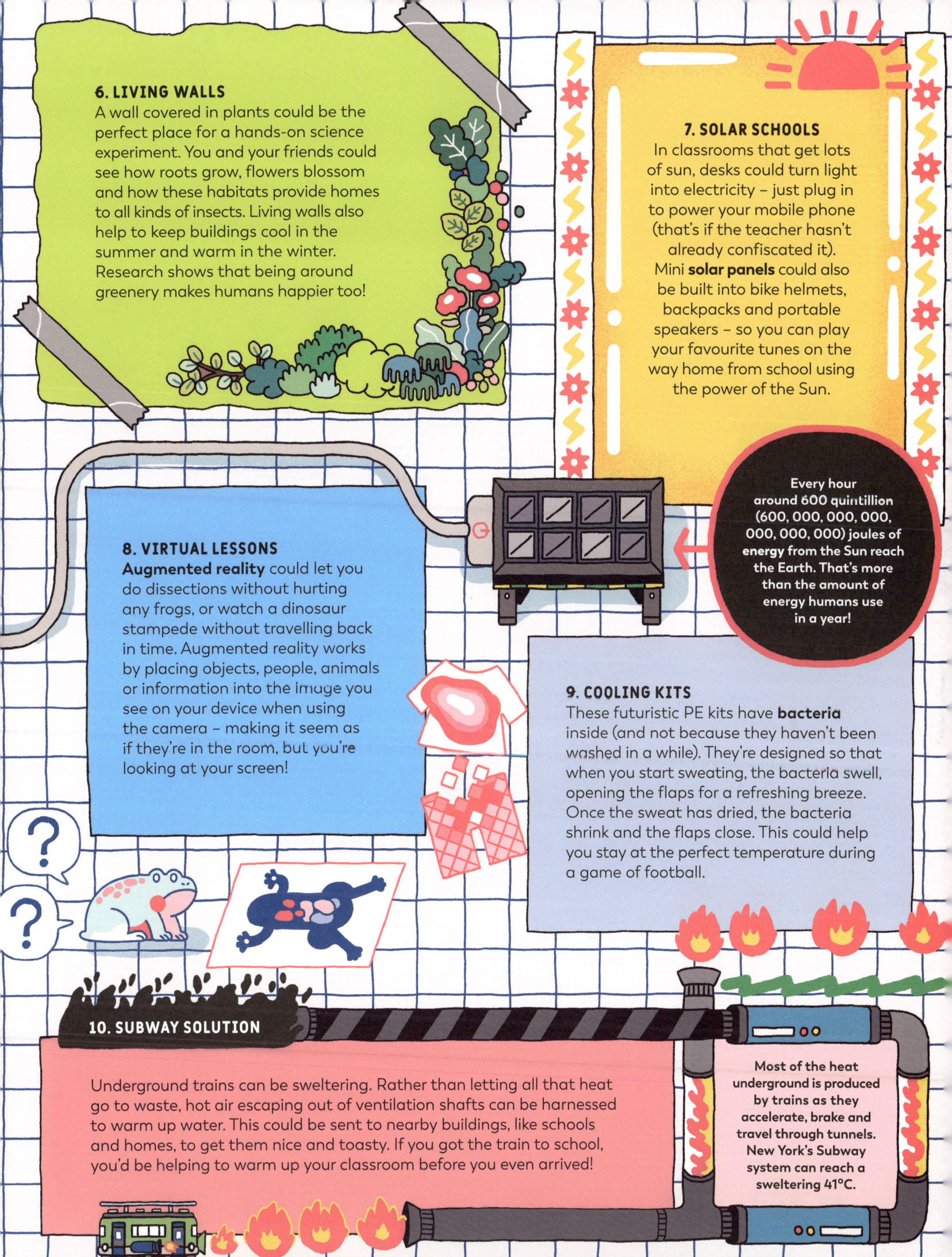

HOT IN HERE

Have you ever sat sweating in a boiling-hot classroom? Or stood shivering in the middle of the playground at lunch? It can be hard to keep cool in the summer and warm in the winter without using loads of **energy**. Generating heat, or getting rid of it, is a challenge that scientists and engineers have tried to find a solution for in lots of different ways.

WHAT'S THE PROBLEM?

Humans use heat in hundreds of ways. Just think about your school day. Classrooms need to be kept at the right temperature, then there's hot showers to take after PE and lunch to warm in the canteen. A whole lot of heat is needed in schools, and at home the hunt for heat continues as we boil kettles and turn up radiators.

It isn't just daily activities which involve heat. It's needed to make all kinds of things from cars and computers, to plastic bags and playgrounds. Heat has even been used to produce this book. Creating warmth takes **energy**, but as most of our energy comes from burning **fossil fuels**, scientists are on the search for new ways to create heat.

NUCLEAR FUSION

Like all stars, in its core the Sun smashes **hydrogen nuclei** into each other. When hydrogen nuclei fuse together, this creates **helium** and releases **energy**. Bottling this energy back on Earth would be brilliant, but it's proving tricky for scientists to work out how.

The Sun's huge size makes slamming particles together easier. It is seriously massive, and all of that mass is compressing together under the force of **gravity**. This intense pressure makes the Sun extremely hot. It can reach 15 million degrees Celsius at the core. With very high pressures and temperatures, hydrogen nuclei are pushed together and have enough energy to overcome their repulsive forces, allowing them to fuse. Have you ever tried pushing the same poles of magnets together? It's a bit like that – you need to put in a lot of extra work to force them to meet!

The amount of heat produced by a single gram of fusion material would be able to boil a swimming pool!

TOTALLY SMASHING

Back here on Earth, trying to create **nuclear fusion** will take some formidable physics. As we can't replicate the Sun's colossal mass, the temperature inside reactors would need to be around a hundred million degrees Celsius. Scientists are already working on experiments, but it's a hard nut to crack – and could still be another thirty years away. Still, if we ever manage to recreate the science inside a star, we'll have a virtually limitless source of carbon-free energy.

STAYING COOL

As the planet warms, we'll also have to design different techniques for cooling ourselves and our surroundings down. No one wants to turn into a big puddle of sweat during an assembly. Unfortunately, air conditioners are **energy**-draining devices, so engineers are going back to the drawing board to find some cooler alternatives.

NO SWEAT OFF MY BACK

Futuristic clothes could copy the natural wonders of **biodiversity** to lower our body temperatures! Different animals have different ways of keeping cool. Elephants flap their ears, pigs roll in mud and vultures ... poo on their legs. You'd look pretty weird attempting any of these methods (and probably get chucked out of school for some!). Thankfully, humans also have a trick up our sleeves – sweating. The moisture your body produces **evaporates** from your skin, taking a bit of heat with it.

Mimicking this process, this high-tech T-shirt is covered in a material a bit like a sponge. While you're busy playing football or hockey, the material can slowly evaporate the water from sweat as air passes over it – keeping you cool. The T-shirt's lining is waterproof so you don't get drenched too!

The human body has up to five million sweat glands. Most are on the palms of your hands and soles of your feet!

FREEZEY-PEASY

On a hot day, there's nothing better than a cold drink, but to get one on the go, your fridge has to run all day and night. As well as using loads of power, fridges contain **greenhouse gases** that escape into the **atmosphere** when the appliances get chucked away. So, unlike the salads inside them, refrigerators aren't very green. Coming up with a more environmentally friendly design has proved challenging, even for some of the world's brightest minds (physicist Albert Einstein once gave it a go). But now engineers have invented a machine with futuristic tech inside that can chill a can of fizzy drink within a minute. It's like an anti-kettle! This would be perfect for replacing cooling systems in vending machines. It doesn't solve the problem of big refrigerators, but it's a start.

GOING POTTY

Occasionally, teachers can have some good ideas too... One teacher from Nigeria called Mohammed Bah Abba invented the pot-in-pot refrigerator, which can stay cool without any electricity. Like sweating, Mohammed's fridge uses **evaporating** liquid to draw away heat. Why not try making one for keeping packed lunches fresh until break?

1. Take two big clay pots – one smaller than the other (make sure to plug up any holes in the bottom).

2. Put the smaller clay pot inside the bigger one and fill the gap with sand.

3. Soak the sand with plenty of water. You'll need to keep topping up the water so the sand doesn't dry out.

4. Put your items for cooling inside the smaller pot and then cover just that pot with a damp cloth. You have made your own eco-fridge!

IN THE PARK

Scientists have shown that spending time among trees, flowers and grass is great for your health. These areas also provide a home for all kinds of creatures, as well as sucking up CO_2 and producing **oxygen**. Hopefully in the future there will be plenty more parks filled with gadgets and gizmos to help protect the nature around us.

6 **TREE TURBINES**   7 **PLAN BEE**   8 **FISHY FILM**   9 **POLLINATION ARMY**

1. MOSS MONITOR

Instead of fancy equipment, scientists want to use moss to test how clean the air is. Mosses get their water and nutrients from the **atmosphere** around them. Studies have shown that mosses absorb pollution in the air too. It can affect their shape, size and colour. So checking up on the health of moss can tell scientists how foul or fresh the air really is.

2. SPUD SPOON

Plastic cutlery is convenient and strong but after just one use, billions of knives, forks and spoons are chucked away each year. One alternative to this is potato cutlery. With ingenious engineering, potatoes can be transformed into picnic utensils. When lunch is finished, stick the spoon in the ground and it will decompose and provide nutrients for the soil.

3. ROADS FOR TOADS

As the globe gets hotter, lots of animals will have to move to cooler climates. To help them on their way, we'll need to create worldwide 'wildlife corridors', connected through parks and cities. These vast pathways would be full of local trees and plants. Cut off from human interference, the networks would give animals a safe place to live and travel.

4. POWER PLAY

With this kite you produce power while you play. When it's flying in the breeze, fans in the kite turn a mini-generator, creating electricity. The electricity then runs down the string (with wires inside), into a battery. These kites are usually used out in the ocean where it's windier.

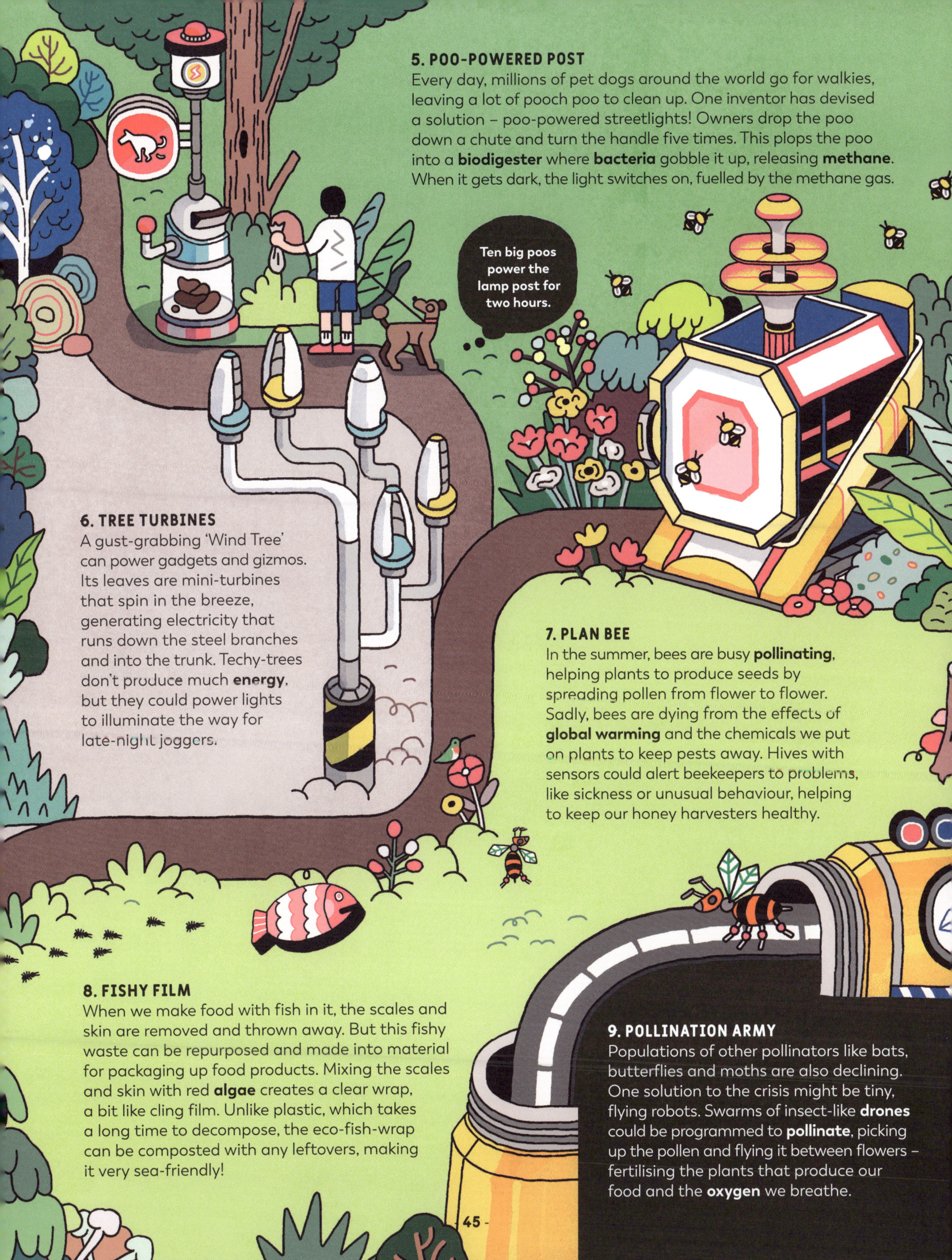

5. POO-POWERED POST

Every day, millions of pet dogs around the world go for walkies, leaving a lot of pooch poo to clean up. One inventor has devised a solution – poo-powered streetlights! Owners drop the poo down a chute and turn the handle five times. This plops the poo into a **biodigester** where **bacteria** gobble it up, releasing **methane**. When it gets dark, the light switches on, fuelled by the methane gas.

Ten big poos power the lamp post for two hours.

6. TREE TURBINES

A gust-grabbing 'Wind Tree' can power gadgets and gizmos. Its leaves are mini-turbines that spin in the breeze, generating electricity that runs down the steel branches and into the trunk. Techy-trees don't produce much **energy**, but they could power lights to illuminate the way for late-night joggers.

7. PLAN BEE

In the summer, bees are busy **pollinating**, helping plants to produce seeds by spreading pollen from flower to flower. Sadly, bees are dying from the effects of **global warming** and the chemicals we put on plants to keep pests away. Hives with sensors could alert beekeepers to problems, like sickness or unusual behaviour, helping to keep our honey harvesters healthy.

8. FISHY FILM

When we make food with fish in it, the scales and skin are removed and thrown away. But this fishy waste can be repurposed and made into material for packaging up food products. Mixing the scales and skin with red **algae** creates a clear wrap, a bit like cling film. Unlike plastic, which takes a long time to decompose, the eco-fish-wrap can be composted with any leftovers, making it very sea-friendly!

9. POLLINATION ARMY

Populations of other pollinators like bats, butterflies and moths are also declining. One solution to the crisis might be tiny, flying robots. Swarms of insect-like **drones** could be programmed to **pollinate**, picking up the pollen and flying it between flowers – fertilising the plants that produce our food and the **oxygen** we breathe.

BRILLIANT BIODIVERSITY

We call the assortment of animals and plants on the planet its **biodiversity**. This biodiversity has evolved over millions of years, solving problems from how best to survive desert heat or Arctic cold, to staying safe from predators and catching prey. There's an incredible amount we can learn from these amazing adaptations. If we look after nature, it will help us in return.

WHAT'S THE PROBLEM?

There are an estimated 8.7 million plant and animal species on Earth but scientists have calculated that one million species are now threatened with **extinction**. Species sometimes die out for natural reasons, but often it's because humans are harming their **ecosystems**. Ecosystems are a bit like a spider's web of interconnected threads – everything is dependent on something else. Imagine a tree – its leaves are home to insects, which birds eat. The birds' droppings help **fungi** at the bottom of the trunk grow. The fungi are eaten by badgers who burrow among the tree's roots. If you disturb one part of the ecosystem, everything changes! But **biodiversity** is in crisis, so, to slow down extinction, we need to take care of the environment and everything in it.

TREE TSUNAMI

Rainforests are home to an estimated more than half of all the world's plants and animals, including poison dart frogs, pink river dolphins and Goliath birdeater spiders. Rainforests suck up and store vast amounts of carbon, reducing the impacts of **global warming**. Plus, many of the plants found in rainforests can be used to make medicines.

The world's largest tropical rainforest is the Amazon, which covers 6.7 million square kilometres. The Amazon is so big that its trees are able to produce their own rainfall and cause clouds to form above the canopy. This helps to keep it moist and cool. Unfortunately, lots of the Amazon has been cut down, destroying habitats. This deforestation is also pushing the Amazon rainforest over its 'tipping point', where it can no longer maintain its own wet and humid climate. If this happens, it could quickly degrade into a hot and dry savannah.

But, turning this problem on its head, scientists have calculated that reforestation is a great way to tackle damage caused to the Amazon rainforest, and **climate change** more widely. All we need to do is stop chopping and start planting! By growing millions of trees we can reinstate rainforest **ecosystems**, keep them healthy and build the greenest carbon-capture technology out there. All over the globe, countries are planning on sowing more seeds. Pakistan has already been busy doing just that, and in three years the country managed to plant more than a billion trees.

NATURE'S TIPS

While new ideas are needed to protect our planet's **biodiversity**, smart inventions can also be sparked by admiring the brilliance of biology. Nature is ingenious, and it's already found solutions to all kinds of issues! Taking inspiration from nature is known as **biomimicry**.

After being swallowed by toads, bombardier beetles can fire their toxic chemicals — causing the toads to vomit the beetles back up alive!

BOMBARDED BY BEETLES

Inside the tiny bodies of bombardier beetles is a complicated chemistry set and some extraordinary bioengineering that means they can fire rapid bursts of hot, toxic liquid from their backsides – useful for fighting off predators! In the beetle's abdomen are two chemicals stored in separate sections. Mixing them together causes a chemical reaction that produces intense heat, allowing them to send out the fiery spray. Mimicking this amazing anatomy, scientists are working out better ways to get medicine into the body, like creating new kinds of inhalers for asthma sufferers. Engineers might also get ideas for fire extinguishers, which could send out a jet of large droplets or a finer mist, depending on what kind of fire needs to be put out.

WATER-SAVING SCUTTLER

The head-stander beetle, which lives in the dry Namib Desert, is also a source of inspiration. To survive, the beetle gathers water from the morning fog that floats across the dunes. Facing the breeze with its bum tipped up, tiny droplets collect around special bumps on the beetle's wings. Once the droplets have built up, they roll along water-repelling troughs on the beetle's back – straight into its mouth! Using this geometry, engineers are designing 'condensers' – devices that can pull water out of air, providing another source of H_2O in hot and humid places.

Scientists have shown slime mould can even solve mazes!

SUPER-SMART SLIME

Slime mould isn't a plant, animal or a type of fungus, but a different kind of organism altogether. Slime moulds can be made up of one single cell, growing up to a few square metres in size. Despite not having brains, they are also experts at finding the best routes between food sources. First, arm-like tendrils ooze outwards to explore the surroundings. Then, the slime mould works out the most direct routes between meals and turns into a network of tubes.

Slime mould could show us the most efficient routes for travel networks, shuttling us to the park in super-quick time. Scientists have tested this by seeing if slime would mimic a rail system in Japan. They arranged porridge oats imitating the location of cities around the capital, Tokyo. The size of the oat pile reflected the population of the city, so more oats for bigger cities. Amazingly, the slime mould built a network of food-carrying tubes out of itself, which was similar to the real rail system that engineers had spent years designing and building! Next time we need to create an efficient transport system we should ask the slime mould first.

ON THE FARM

There are over 7.6 billion people on our planet. That's a lot of mouths to feed. Growing enough food to keep everyone full up and healthy, while caring for the environment, is a gargantuan task. To do it, we're going to need some seriously futuristic farming.

1. SPY IN THE SKY

Farmers are increasingly using **drones** to spy on their land. Equipped with cameras and sensors, drones buzz over fields checking if they need water and looking for signs of fungal infections or pests. Engineers have even designed drones that can shoot seeds and nutrients into the soil.

2. FORESTS OF FOOD

One day, farms might look a lot more like forests. Rather than clearing land for crops, some pioneering farmers are growing berry bushes, nut trees and leafy greens all together! Edible forests take less work than traditional farms and, with hundreds of species of plants, they are also less vulnerable to disease and **climate change**. Their **biodiversity** means food forests create a natural **ecosystem**.

3. WEED WONDERS

We might need to think twice before attacking weeds with a trowel. Wild plants that grow without being cultivated by gardeners or farmers tend to be more resistant to diseases, pests and weather events like storms and floods caused by **global warming**. Scientists are working on **cross-breeding** our crops with wild plants so they get some of these useful traits.

4. SKY FARMS

Farms usually stretch out across the land, but what if they reached upwards instead? So-called vertical farms could be the perfect solution for urban environments with limited growing space. Inside disused factories or even in blocks of flats, layers of plants can be stacked on top of each other. Vertical farms can provide exactly the right amount of water, light and nutrients – hardly wasting a thing.

5. FISHY FEEDING

'Aquaponics' sounds complicated, but it's actually super simple. Fish are kept in a tank and fed. Then, they do what all animals do – poo and wee. The wastewater is pumped into growing beds above, where **bacteria** turn the fish waste into nutrients. Plants' roots absorb the nutrients and the filtered water is sent back to the tank below.

6. LIVESTOCK SENSORS

From collars for cows to ankle bracelets for chickens, wearable sensors can monitor whether farm animals are eating, sleeping or moving around and even measure their temperatures. This helps farmers keep track of the health, activity and behaviour of their livestock.

7. ROBO-FARMERS

Farms take a lot of looking after, from sowing seeds to watering crops. Luckily, robots are on hand to help. Engineers have designed robots that can pootle around farms and perform different jobs, from picking strawberries to planting vegetables. As well as never needing to sleep, agri-bots can make farming more precise, reducing waste, water and the need for pest-killing chemicals.

8. GREEN-MANSIONS

Ginormous greenhouses spanning as far as the eye can see could one day be a common view across the countryside. Acting like vast heat traps, conditions inside mean plants like sweet potatoes, peppers and melons would thrive. In cities, enormous transparent domes called 'biomes' could perform the same trick. With added **solar panels** and smart sensors, they might just be the farms of the future.

9. ORGANIC PLANET

Next to Earth, Mars is the most habitable planet in our solar system. Scientists are busy replicating Martian conditions to work out how to cultivate food there. With a possible population of 11 billion people on Earth by 2100, there's a chance that some of us might choose to venture into space and make a new home on the red planet. We'll need to know how to grow food in alien conditions if we do!

LOOKING AFTER THE LAND

We use around 38% of Earth's land for agriculture. In creating this space for our food, we clear away wild habitats which remove **carbon dioxide** from the **atmosphere**, clean our air and water and support the world's **biodiversity**. As **climate change** brings more weather extremes, like blistering heatwaves and droughts that dry out the ground, the quality of our land is only going to get worse, so we need to start looking after it now.

WHAT'S THE PROBLEM?

Humans need to eat, and that requires lots of land for crops and cattle. For large-scale agriculture, the space is often created by deforestation or removing other natural terrains. In most cases, once the land is cleared it's intensively farmed – using huge machines and chemicals to grow one chosen crop and get rid of any other plants and insects there. This slowly degrades the land, removing nutrients from the soil and wiping out **ecosystems**.

REWIND AND REWILD

While we work out how to produce food in smaller areas, we can also devise ways to make our land healthier too. By recreating forests, mangroves and marshes, we can do a lot of good for our planet and help the animals who depend on it. Reinstating plants and creatures (then letting them do their own thing) is known as 'rewilding'.

In the UK, beavers have been released back into the countryside. Scientists found that where these rodents lived, frogspawn increased and insects and plants flourished. The beavers' dams even helped to clean the local water and reduce flood risk! Bigger than beavers, bison have been reintroduced to the mountains of Romania. Bison roam and graze on grasses – making room for other plants and spreading nutrients and seeds by dropping dung across the land!

A MAMMOTH TASK

Some scientists even want to bring woolly mammoths back from **extinction**. The aim is to have these Ice Age giants roaming the Arctic tundra once again. Vast areas of ground across the Arctic have been frozen since the Ice Age. As the Earth heats up, this **permafrost** is starting to melt, allowing the frozen plants trapped inside to finally rot, releasing **carbon dioxide** and **methane**. This is where woolly mammoths plod into the picture. Like the bison, by stomping around, they would trample trees and shrubs which absorb sunlight (and therefore heat), and instead encourage grasses to grow which reflect more light (keeping things cooler). Squashing the snow as they lumber across the Arctic also helps the freezing winter temperatures penetrate deep into the permafrost soil, so it stays icy cold.

Using woolly mammoth carcasses that have been preserved in ice, scientists are studying their **DNA** to one day recreate some of their **genes** in the lab. The plan is to combine the genes with a close living relative, the Asian elephant, and create an elephant-mammoth hybrid, or 'mammophant'.

TAKE A BREAK

While we wait for woolly mammoths to reappear, farmers are also looking for new ways to restore land and revitalize unhealthy soils. Thankfully, alongside bringing back wildlife, another way to help what's living above and below ground is to do absolutely nothing. It's all about chilling out to help out.

LAZY FOR GOOD

Without us interfering, nature tends to find its own way – and usually takes over too. The owners of Knepp Estate, a farm in the UK, have let their land be reclaimed by wildlife. After intensively farming it for years, the land wasn't fit for growing crops or grazing animals any more so the farmers decided to let it heal in its own way. Soon, a wide range of trees, grasses and flowers returned – as well as rare birds like peregrine falcons. Cows and pigs wander wherever they like, eating whatever they find, so the farmers have to do hardly anything to raise their livestock! Being a bit lazy (for a good cause) doesn't need to happen on a huge scale either. If you have a garden, perhaps you could persuade your parents to let a small part of it turn wild.

GIVING EARTH SOME SPACE

One way to leave Earth alone would be for lots of us to relocate – to space! A popular idea is to go up in a pair of O'Neill cylinders, two twenty-mile-long tubes, rotating in opposite directions, each attached to a ring of farming pods that look a bit like giant bicycle wheels. This off-Earth settlement would need to spin super-fast in order to pin the inhabitants to the tubes' floor (as there wouldn't be any **gravity** to keep things down). By moving citizens to a space-cylinder, the land we use for agriculture would have time to regenerate. In particular, it's the stuff beneath our feet that needs a break from being farmed...

SAVE OUR SOILS

Under the surface, soil is teeming with life. A gram of the stuff contains billions of microbes, like **bacteria**, viruses and **fungi**. All of this life – as well as bigger, soil-dwelling creatures like worms and ants – make mud a brilliant foundation for growing things, including around 95% of our food!

The problem is, farming can damage or even destroy soil **ecosystems**. When soil is in a bad condition it struggles to absorb water and spread nutrients around, so things above ground struggle to grow. To monitor the health of their soils, farmers can use satellites floating in space to spot warning signs – like if it's too wet or too dry. On the ground, people can use sensors to test how acidic soil is (acid is what makes a lemon taste sour), its texture and temperature. This information could be shared on special soil monitoring apps, to keep track of agriculture across the globe.

AT THE BEACH

A trip to the beach can be a perfect way to spend a bright summer's day. Sun, sea, sand ... and often quite a lot of rubbish too! But there are plenty of ways we can clean up our beaches and protect marine life. From litter-munching monsters to houses built with bottles, we can take our heads out of the sand and start being ocean eco-warriors.

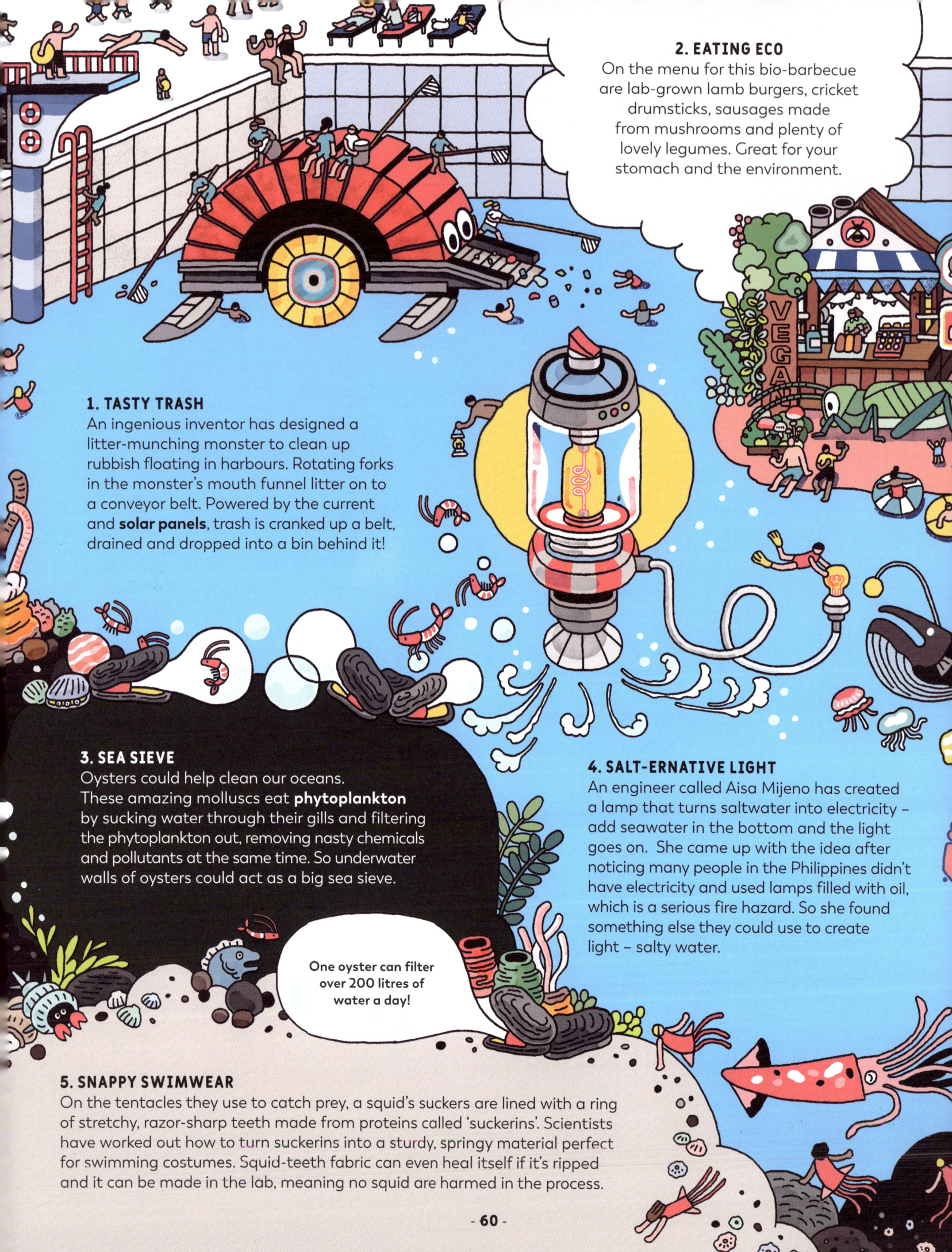

2. EATING ECO

On the menu for this bio-barbecue are lab-grown lamb burgers, cricket drumsticks, sausages made from mushrooms and plenty of lovely legumes. Great for your stomach and the environment.

1. TASTY TRASH

An ingenious inventor has designed a litter-munching monster to clean up rubbish floating in harbours. Rotating forks in the monster's mouth funnel litter on to a conveyor belt. Powered by the current and **solar panels**, trash is cranked up a belt, drained and dropped into a bin behind it!

3. SEA SIEVE

Oysters could help clean our oceans. These amazing molluscs eat **phytoplankton** by sucking water through their gills and filtering the phytoplankton out, removing nasty chemicals and pollutants at the same time. So underwater walls of oysters could act as a big sea sieve.

One oyster can filter over 200 litres of water a day!

4. SALT-ERNATIVE LIGHT

An engineer called Aisa Mijeno has created a lamp that turns saltwater into electricity – add seawater in the bottom and the light goes on. She came up with the idea after noticing many people in the Philippines didn't have electricity and used lamps filled with oil, which is a serious fire hazard. So she found something else they could use to create light – salty water.

5. SNAPPY SWIMWEAR

On the tentacles they use to catch prey, a squid's suckers are lined with a ring of stretchy, razor-sharp teeth made from proteins called 'suckerins'. Scientists have worked out how to turn suckerins into a sturdy, springy material perfect for swimming costumes. Squid-teeth fabric can even heal itself if it's ripped and it can be made in the lab, meaning no squid are harmed in the process.

6. SMASHING SAND

Sand isn't just found at the beach – it's found in walls, windows and even roads. We use colossal amounts of the stuff, more than enough to build thousands of full-sized castles. A glass-bottle-eating vending machine can pulverise glass into tiny pieces, creating artificial sand. This helps preserve the environment by saving sand and recycling old bottles.

The rubber left on old tyres can also be turned into a material to make volleyballs.

7. IN THE NET

Over 600,000 tonnes of fishing equipment ends up in the ocean every year. Animals often get stuck in the nets, so an initiative called the Good Net Project is gathering them and turning them into something new – volleyball nets!

8. CALLING ALL CREATURES

As **climate change** warms the oceans, coral reefs are turning white and dying This is called **coral bleaching**. The incredible array of creatures living in the reefs are forced to abandon them. To tempt creatures back to dead coral in Australia's Great Barrier Reef, scientists blasted sounds of healthy reefs through waterproof speakers. The noise of snapping shrimp and grunting fish persuaded many critters to return, which the scientists hope will support the recovery of the coral.

The Great Barrier Reef is the world's largest coral reef system, home to 1,500 species of fish.

Corals might look like underwater bushes, but they're actually animals. Corals are made up of many smaller individual coral organisms, called 'polyps.'

9. HUNTING MICROPLASTICS

Microplastics might be less than five millimetres in size, but millions of them end up in the ocean, causing trouble for marine life. When she was twelve, aspiring engineer Anna Du came up with a plan. Anna built an underwater robot that hunts down where microplastics have accumulated. Using sensors and software, her submersible vehicle roves around, identifying patterns, colours and shapes that could be microplastics so they can one day be collected or studied.

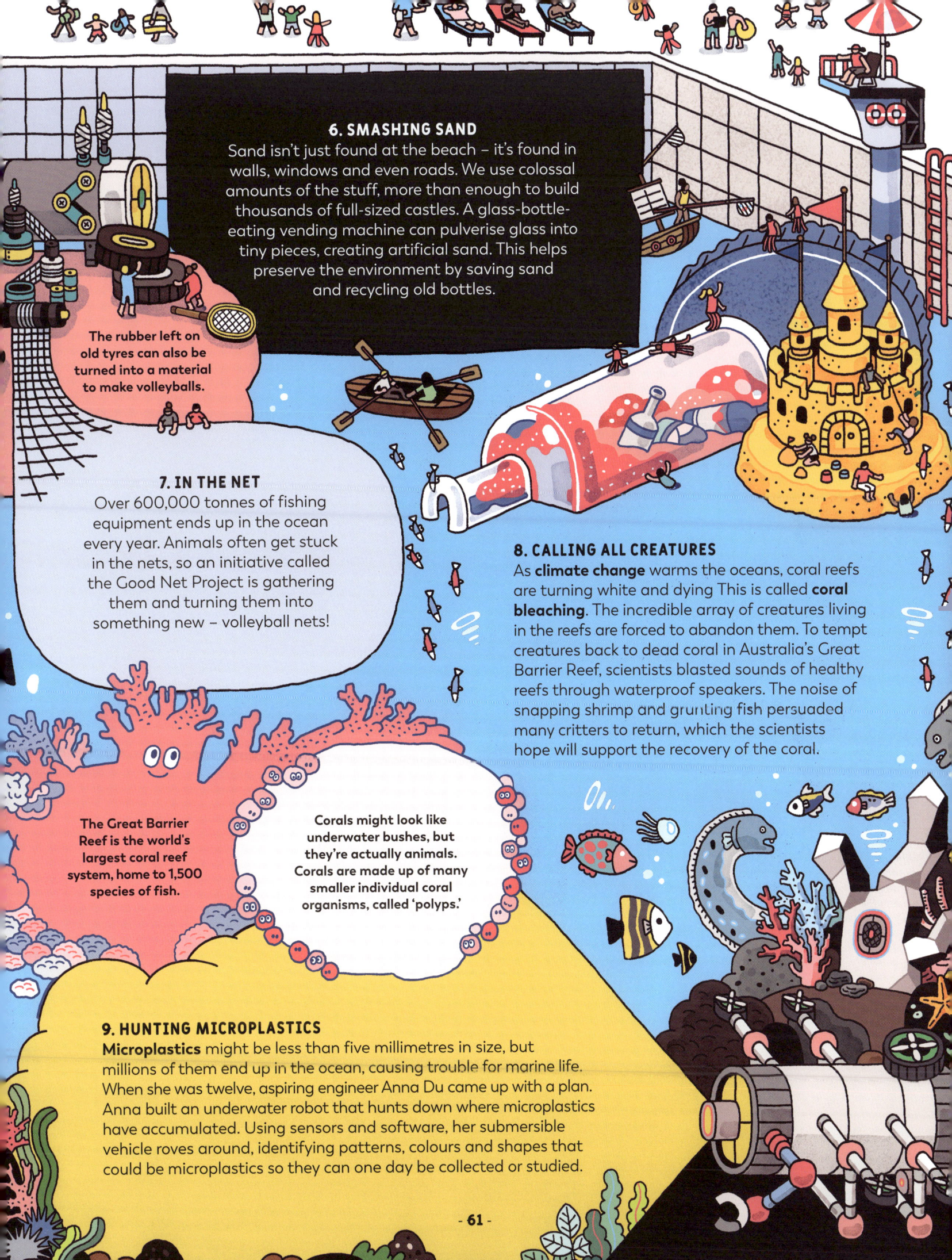

WASTE NOT WANT NOT

Humans have a bad habit of throwing things away. From water bottles to old socks with holes in them, lots of this litter ends up in the ocean. Rather than jam-packing our planet with junk, we need to come up with ways we can recycle and reuse our mess. One of the main culprits is plastic.

WHAT'S THE PROBLEM?

We have got an enormous, gargantuan, humongous problem with plastic. Since its invention in 1855, humanity has wasted over six billion tonnes of it. That's enough to build 1,000 Great Pyramids of Giza! But have you ever wondered where it goes once it's been thrown away? According to scientists, we've only recycled 9% of it. The rest is either sent to landfill, burned or shipped to other countries to deal with! No one wants pyramids of plastic, so we need to turn it into something new...

HOUSE IN A BOTTLE

Fill some old plastic bottles with sand or dirt, stack them on their sides, bind them with mud or even cow poo – and you'll be halfway to building a house. Packed plastic bottles are cheaper and stronger than traditional bricks. Plus, they're great insulators, keeping the inside of a house cool when the Sun is hot. Bottle buildings have been constructed across the world in India, Colombia and Nigeria.

POO-PROOF ROOF

Babies are poo and pee machines, going through multiple nappies every day. These plastic nappies are usually chucked straight into the bin, but they could be turned into roof tiles instead! Collected by special recycling plants, first the waste is removed, then the nappies are washed, shredded and dried. All the different materials inside are separated, then the plastic can be recovered and transformed into a material for making roof tiles.

MODERN MATERIALS

As well as using recycled plastic in our buildings, we can also wear it. Fashion moves so quickly we end up chucking loads of it away and as a lot of our clothes are made from plastic, this adds to our problem. Plus, each time we wash our favourite tops and trousers, microfibres are pulled off and swept away into rivers and oceans. Instead of making more and more planet-harming clothes, we could recycle materials and make eco-friendly fashion out of waste.

BOTTLES TO BIKINIS

To turn trash into trunks, first the plastic needs to be washed and shredded into small flakes. The flakes are then melted and turned into plastic pellets. Melting them again, the plastic can be spun into threads to make all kinds of clothes. By creating swimwear from recycled bottles, the plastic might be hitting the ocean waves but it'll be coming back out of the sea with us at the end of the day! Recycled plastic can also be turned into shoes, bags and even the lining of winter jackets to keep the wearer toasty in the snow.

SUSTAINABLE SHOES

Scientists have found a way to make fruity footwear from the fibres of pineapple leaves, a part of the plant that usually goes to waste. Turning the leaves into shoes is a sweet substitute that saves water and land. However, to make the pineapple fabric sturdy, plastic has to be added to the mix. So although they're a step in the right direction, these shoes aren't totally sustainable just yet.

KOMBUCHA CLOTHING

One brainy professor is making shoes, handbags and dresses out of the waste from a drink called kombucha tea. To make the drink, a colony of **bacteria** and yeast, which looks a lot like a slimy pancake, is added to sweetened tea and fermented for a few weeks. Once it's brewed, you're left with a fizzy drink and a slippery film. After drying out the film, the professor, Young-A Lee, realised it was a lot like leather. Since her discovery, she's been running experiments in her lab to try and make the material more waterproof and less liable to rip.

PROCESSED POO

It's possible to produce fabric from cow poo. Cows graze on grass and hay, chomping down a load of it every day. What comes out the other end contains lots of this vegetation. With a bit of chemistry, a substance called 'cellulose' can be extracted out of the poo. Cellulose is part of the building blocks of plant cell walls, so it's pretty tough stuff. The cellulose can then be turned into material for making clothing. By processing the poo this way, the clothes are clean and don't smell at all!

AT HOME

As well as being full of green gadgets, houses could help to reduce the impacts of **global warming** and **climate change** in the future. Built with new materials and designed to keep inhabitants happy while using less **energy**, our dwellings could be the perfect place to start living our best environmental lives...

1. LIVING LIGHT

The **bacteria** found on the suckers of a deep-sea octopus could light our homes! Placed inside this hanging lamp, when the bacteria come into contact with **oxygen**, they make a molecule in their bodies called luciferin, which produces light. To switch the lamp on, you just need to give it a tap and let it wobble. This mixes oxygen with the bacteria and the lamp will start to shine.

A whopping 76% of ocean animals can create their own light, from jellyfish to squid!

2. BACTERIAL BATTERIES

Scientists have discovered that **bacteria** found in our guts and fermenting yogurt can produce electricity. In fact, diarrhoea-inducing bacteria and the bacteria that cause gangrene (a condition where loss of blood supply causes parts of the body to rot and decay) can perform this trick too! One day, we might be able to harness these microbes to power music speakers.

All humans are about 99.9% genetically similar even if we appear different on the surface. Scientists have also found that we have some **genes** similar to those of bananas!

3. SWEET ENERGY SOURCE

Sugar is used as a delicious **energy** source by all kinds of creatures, from humans to ants and hummingbirds (though they prefer flowers' nectar over biscuits!). A sugar-battery mimics the way living organisms get energy from the sweet stuff, serving it up to power electrical devices.

4. GLOWING GREEN

Have you ever seen a glittering glowworm or the flash of a firefly? These amazing animals make luciferin and produce light. By tinkering around with plants' **genes**, scientists managed to get leaves to make luciferin too! These glowing plants could light up your living room – no electricity needed.

5. GLOBAL WORMING

Worms may not make the cuddliest of pets, but they are excellent at eating rubbish from the kitchen, like vegetable trimmings, old fruit and eggshells. Keep them in a container with two parts – one for the worms and compost and another below for the liquid goop that seeps out – and you have yourself a waste-combating wormery.

Farmland adding up to an area bigger than China is used to grow all the food we never end up eating.

In Europe, over 170kg of food per person is wasted each year, but people in sub-Saharan Africa only throw away about 10kg.

6. DRONE POST

In the future, **drone** delivery services could carry packages to your home. By flying directly from shops, drones could save **energy** compared to a van driving around twisty roads. But first we need to make sure they don't disturb birds or bump into buildings, and that they work in all kinds of weather.

7. PLANT BEDS

Scientists are working out ways to grow vegetables and herbs by replacing soil with old mattresses. By soaking foam from mattresses in water mixed with all the nutrients a plant needs, they have been able to get seeds to successfully sprout. Millions of mattresses get thrown away every year, so reusing them to grow food in places where the soil isn't very healthy would be a greener alternative to sleepwalking towards the landfill!

8. PRAWN PACKAGING

Sometimes deliveries are wrapped up in packaging like a pass-the-parcel. Although this keeps the delivery safe from scratches, it uses a lot of plastic that goes in the bin. Sea creatures could give us an environmentally friendly alternative. Crabs, crayfish and shrimp have shells containing a substance called chitin which can be transformed into **biodegradable** packaging material.

9. SCIENCE SOFTWARE

Scientists sometimes need to work out such complicated calculations that even the most powerful computers in the world take months to solve them. To help, we can run special software on our computers at home. The software performs parts of the calculations in the background while we send emails, play games and check social media, allowing us to help solve some of the world's biggest problems without lifting a finger.

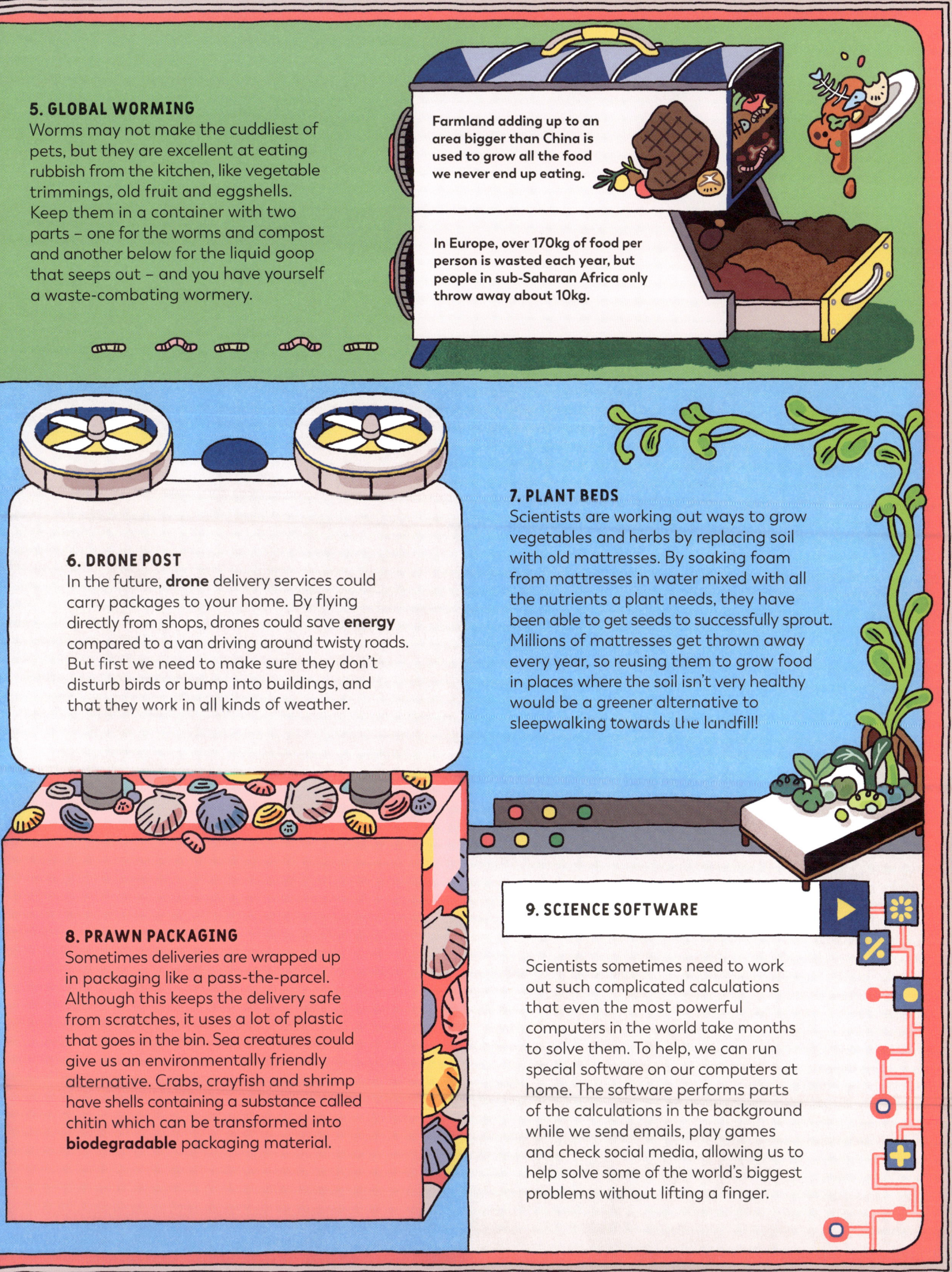

PIONEERING PADS

As the climate changes, our homes need to keep us cool in hot summers, cosy in freezing winters, and be ready for more extreme weather events like floods and snowstorms. As populations grow, we'll have to construct new eco-friendly homes and come up with cutting-edge materials too. But the first conundrum will be where on Earth everyone can go.

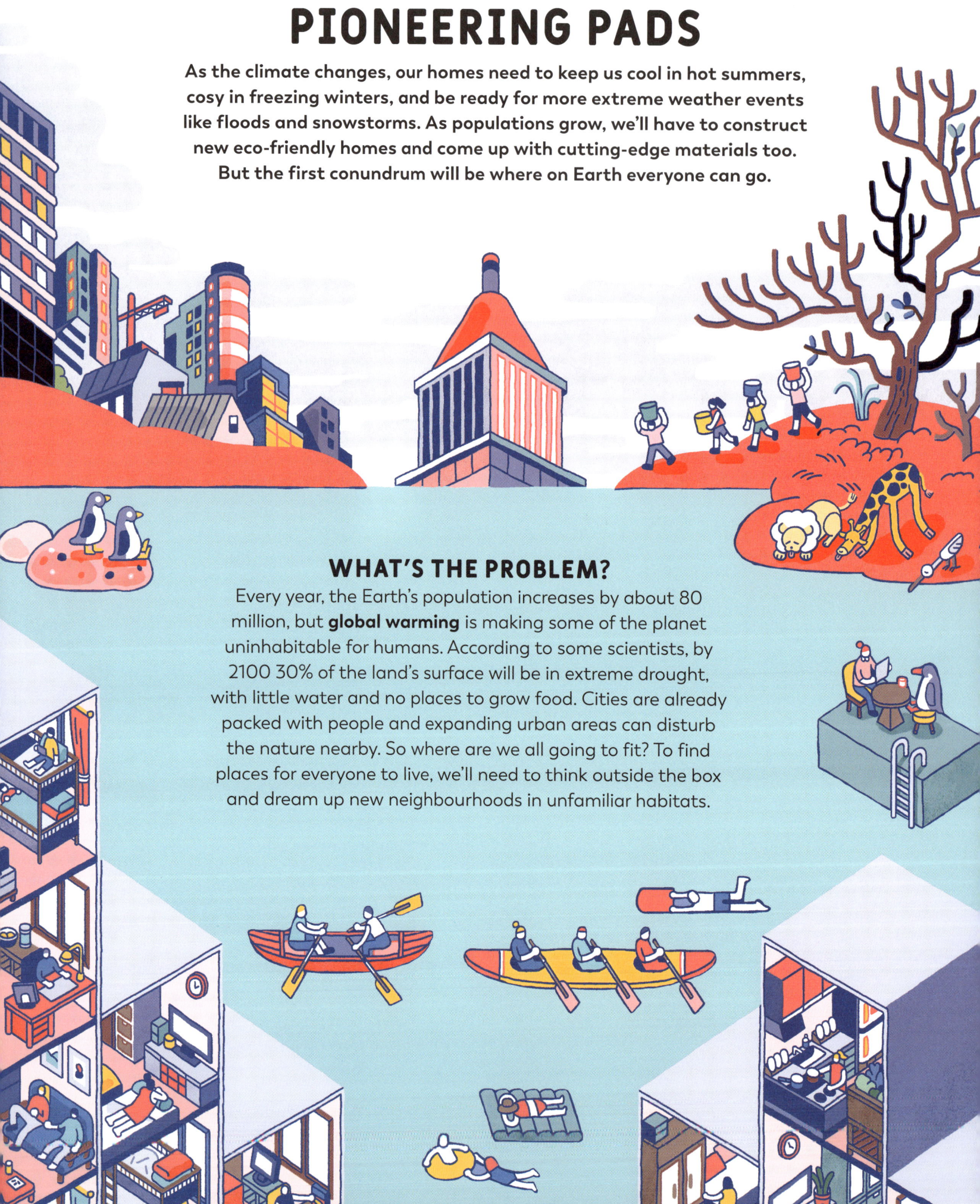

WHAT'S THE PROBLEM?

Every year, the Earth's population increases by about 80 million, but **global warming** is making some of the planet uninhabitable for humans. According to some scientists, by 2100 30% of the land's surface will be in extreme drought, with little water and no places to grow food. Cities are already packed with people and expanding urban areas can disturb the nature nearby. So where are we all going to fit? To find places for everyone to live, we'll need to think outside the box and dream up new neighbourhoods in unfamiliar habitats.

A NEW SEA-VILISATION

One day there might be cities out at sea. Surfing cities could consist of multiple, connected floating platforms anchored to the ocean floor. Houses, shops and even parks could sit on each platform while underwater classrooms and fish farms lie below. Floating cities could harness solar, wave and wind power for **energy**. There are still some technical hurdles to jump before we can dive into amphibious living. Floating cities need to ride out storms without making residents want to puke! This means aquatic abodes might need to be moored near the shore where the waves aren't quite as big.

Even if we drastically cut our carbon emissions right now, by 2100 **climate change** could still cause sea levels to rise by 50cm. They could go up by over 1m if we don't curb **greenhouse gas** emissions. Around 230 million people currently live in areas lying below the 1m-mark. To avoid going underwater, cities will need to be redesigned to avoid flooding.

GOING UNDERGROUND

If you tend to get seasick, there are plenty of other places humans can try inhabiting – like below ground. Don't worry, it's unlikely we'll be scrambling along dark tunnels like moles. Instead, imagine a high-rise building in reverse. Dug deep into the ground, 'earthscrapers' could be designed with spacious rooms and central shafts to let in lots of air and light from above. As well as being a good use of space, temperatures underground tend to be cooler in the summer and warmer in the winter, so there would be less need for **energy**-guzzling heating and air-con systems. Earthscrapers could be particularly useful in places prone to **tornadoes** and storms.

Below Helsinki, the capital city of Finland, is a network of subterranean tunnels that are home to a swimming pool, ice skating rink and sports field.

COMFORTABLE CRIBS

As well as finding new habitats, we also need to build smarter – creating homes that can withstand **climate change** and are eco-friendly. A big part of this will be designing homes that can stay at a comfortable temperature without loads of air conditioning or heating.

LIVING LIKE TERMITES

A surprising source of inspiration are termites. In hot countries around the world, termites erect huge mounds of dirt under the scorching sun. To keep their nests airy and cool, the termites construct a labyrinth of tunnels and vents. These circulate cool and warm air, sucking it in and exhaling it like a giant lung. Copying these critters in human-made buildings could cut down on air conditioning, which consumes a whole lot of **energy**. In fact, a shopping centre in Zimbabwe has already used this principle to keep visitors cool and well-ventilated.

BACTERIA BRICKS

It isn't just how we build houses, but what we build them with. Aside from water, concrete is the most widely used material on Earth but the process of making it is a massive source of **carbon dioxide**. Billions of tonnes of concrete are made every year, and producing just one of its ingredients, cement, accounts for around 8% of global CO_2 emissions.

Concrete might be the best we've got at the minute, but there are other greener materials that could one day take the top spot. One idea scientists are working on is growing bricks with a special kind of **bacteria**. To do this, the bacteria is mixed with gelatine and sand and fed with nutrient-rich water. The bacteria gobble up the nutrients, binding the sand together and building a living brick in the process!

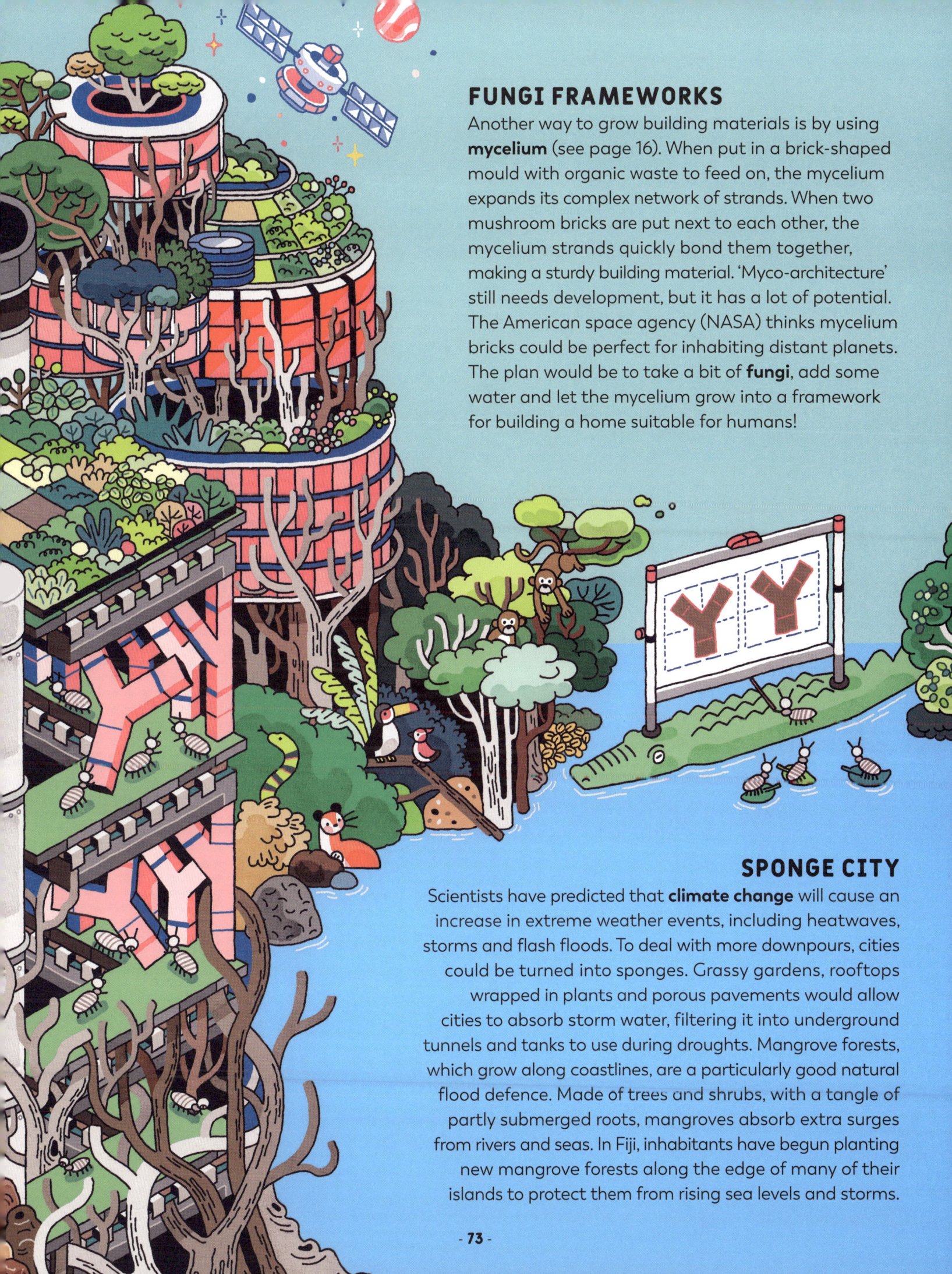

FUNGI FRAMEWORKS

Another way to grow building materials is by using **mycelium** (see page 16). When put in a brick-shaped mould with organic waste to feed on, the mycelium expands its complex network of strands. When two mushroom bricks are put next to each other, the mycelium strands quickly bond them together, making a sturdy building material. 'Myco-architecture' still needs development, but it has a lot of potential. The American space agency (NASA) thinks mycelium bricks could be perfect for inhabiting distant planets. The plan would be to take a bit of **fungi**, add some water and let the mycelium grow into a framework for building a home suitable for humans!

SPONGE CITY

Scientists have predicted that **climate change** will cause an increase in extreme weather events, including heatwaves, storms and flash floods. To deal with more downpours, cities could be turned into sponges. Grassy gardens, rooftops wrapped in plants and porous pavements would allow cities to absorb storm water, filtering it into underground tunnels and tanks to use during droughts. Mangrove forests, which grow along coastlines, are a particularly good natural flood defence. Made of trees and shrubs, with a tangle of partly submerged roots, mangroves absorb extra surges from rivers and seas. In Fiji, inhabitants have begun planting new mangrove forests along the edge of many of their islands to protect them from rising sea levels and storms.

FUTURE THINKING

Problems as big as the climate emergency and **biodiversity** loss require big solutions. We need to think of some creative, pioneering and wacky ideas for solving the crisis and taking care of our planet. Even if they seem peculiar and radical now, in 30 years' time they could be making a revolutionary difference to the world around us. After all, who could have predicted 30 years ago we'd all be walking around with tiny computers in our pockets or kids would be striking from school to get adults to pay attention to global warming?

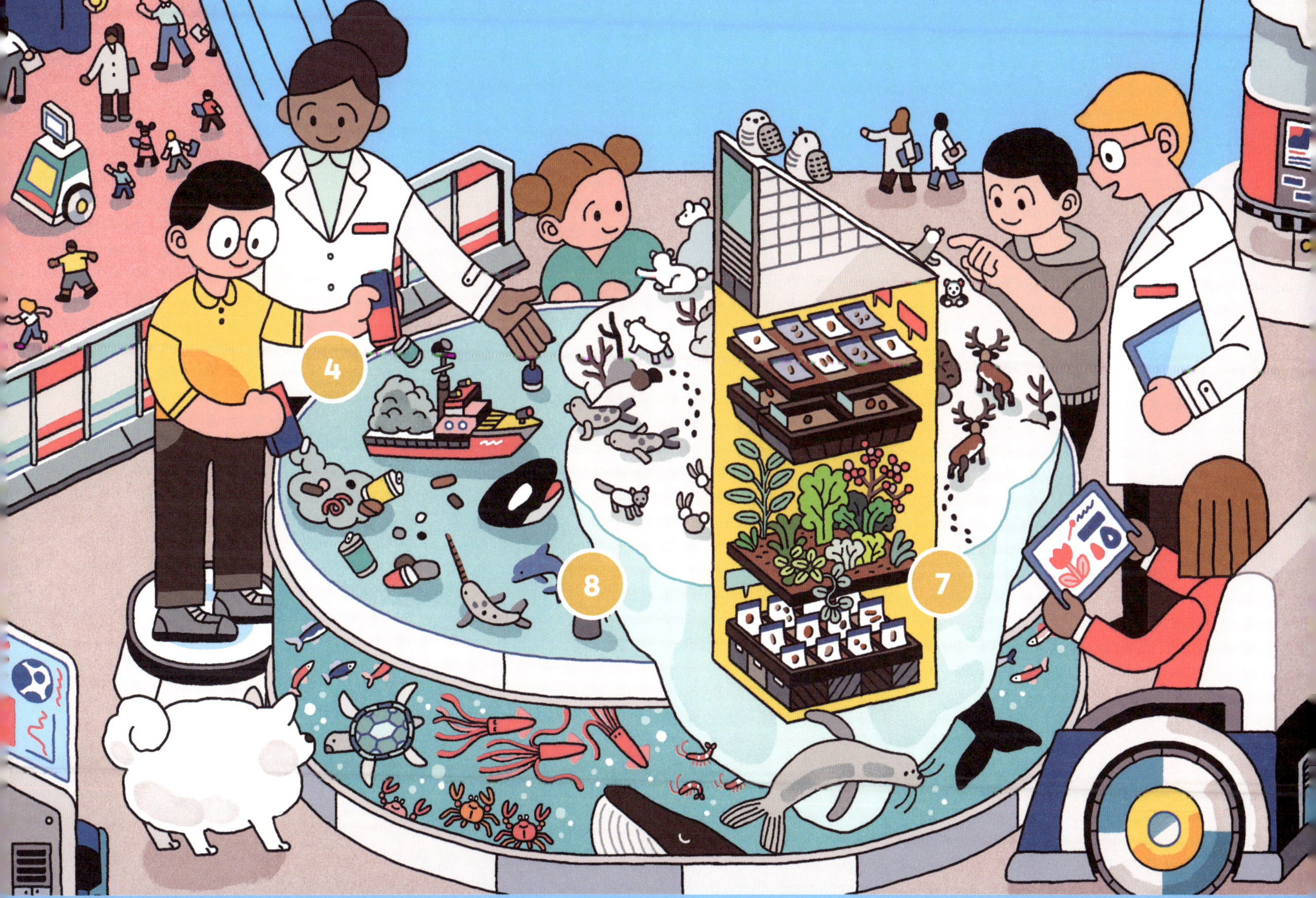

5 NANOBOTS

6 CLOUDS FOR CORALS

7 SAVE OUR SEEDS

8 WONDERFULLY WILD WORLD

1. SPACE ELEVATOR

You need a powerful rocket to blast into space. Making it easier to escape Earth's **gravity**, one day we could ride a space elevator – a cable reaching off into orbit. It would take some incredible engineering, including a huge weight on the other end to pull the cable taut. Currently, there's no material strong enough for the job. Some scientists have suggested dangling a space elevator down from the Moon instead!

2. OUT OF THIS WORLD

Where does the Sun always shine? Space of course! Space-based **solar panels** could collect the Sun's rays and turn them into electricity, without being hindered by clouds, dust and gases in the **atmosphere**. The electricity could be converted into lasers or microwaves and beamed down to Earth.

3. TREMENDOUS TORNADOES

You wouldn't want to encounter a twirling **tornado** in the wild, but what if we could harness its incredible power? Engineers are already trying to make controlled twisters. In the future, they hope to generate swirling vortexes with air warmed by waste heat from factories which would turn turbines to produce electricity.

There could be as many as 50 trillion microplastic particles in the sea – that's 500 times the number of stars in our galaxy!

Irish teenager Fionn Ferreira came up with the idea of capturing **microplastics** with magnets when he spotted rocks covered in tiny bits of plastic while out kayaking.

4. TEENSY-WEENSY TRASH

To fish **microplastics** (see page 61) out of the sea we could try oil and magnetite powder (crushed iron rocks). Adding oil to our oceans sounds like a very bad idea, but oil attracts plastic and they stick together. By mixing in magnetite powder, this chemical cocktail would form a magnetic liquid that could be lifted out using a massive magnet! Although the technique has been tried in laboratory beakers, it'll take much more work before we can add oil to oceans safely.

5. NANOBOTS
Imagine robots so tiny they could travel around the human body or grab pollution particles out of the air. Known as nanobots, scientists are already working on creating minuscule machines ten thousand times smaller than the thickness of this page. Although fully functioning bots are some way off, one day they might be all around us, keeping us and our environment healthy.

Earth's orbit has over 128 million bits of junk whizzing around in it, from broken satellites to fragments from old rockets. To clean up, scientists are developing futuristic space grippers, nets and harpoons.

7. SAVE OUR SEEDS
On a tiny Norwegian island not too far from Greenland, there is a strange building sticking out of the snow. Inside are millions of seeds from all over the world, sent there to help protect plants from natural or man-made disasters. If a crop ever dies, seeds can be collected and sowed again, saving the plant from **extinction**.

6. CLOUDS FOR CORALS
As seas warm up around the world, coral reefs are turning white and dying (see page 61). Scientists have been trying to keep the corals cool, providing them with extra shade by spraying microscopic beads of seawater into the air above reefs. The water then **evaporates**, leaving tiny salt crystals. These salt crystals mix with low-lying clouds, helping the clouds to grow bigger and cast a cooling shadow.

8. WONDERFULLY WILD WORLD
One way of caring for our planet could be to turn half the Earth into a ginormous nature reserve and keep 50% of our planet in its natural state. We could start by looking after the places that are still undamaged by humans, slowly expanding them with help from indigenous and local communities. Then, we could try to join up these areas with vast networks of land for animals to move through. This will mean plenty of us getting used to living a lot closer to nature, and nurturing it too.

FUTURE-PROOF

Scientists have calculated the global average temperature is likely to increase by at least two degrees Celsius by 2100 but could go up as much as five. If humanity takes control of its **fossil-fuel**-guzzling, tree-chopping, plastic-using ways, we can reduce the rate of **climate change** and save many of our planet's habitats. If we carry on as we are, we will face some serious consequences, so it's probably a good idea to start planning some ways to future-proof the planet.

WHAT'S THE PROBLEM?

It's hard to predict what Earth will look like in the future. What we do know is that it will be a more challenging place to live. Thankfully, as you've discovered in this book, there are plenty of things we can do to slow these changes down and make sure it can support life for years to come. Still, people are wondering how to prepare for an uncertain future, and in some cases, they're even preparing for the worst-case scenario.

When humans intrude on nature, like converting land for agriculture, we come into contact with new viruses and **bacteria** that can move from animals to humans, known as zoonotic diseases. The more we damage **ecosystems** and encroach on habitats, the more likely we are to catch something nasty.

HUNKER IN A BUNKER

Hidden in top-secret locations, so-called 'doomsday bunkers' look like small concrete sheds. Inside, however, they descend deep into the ground, and are filled with everything humans need to survive, including supplies of food and water, seeds for growing crops and comfy beds. The plan for these bunkers is to escape from the problems on the surface, such as extreme weather events or diseases spreading around the world, until the danger blows over. Bunkers are often luxuriously kitted out with cinemas and even swimming pools. The trouble is, only a few people can fit in these shelters, which isn't very fair to everyone else!

SPACE-RACING HOME

Another option would be to escape Earth and head off into space. We could do this either by getting in a giant spacecraft (see page 56) or settling on a new planet. The only problem: the planets in our solar system aren't suited to supporting human life. Our best option is Mars. The day length there is an extra 37 minutes long and the average temperature is -63 degrees Celsius. This means the conditions on the red planet are much closer to those on Earth compared to our nearest neighbours, Mercury and Venus. However, as there's no liquid water or **oxygen** on the surface, humans would still have to build bio-bunkers that produced all their own air, H_2O and food. The real question is, why go to Mars at all? If we work out how to create these kinds of biospheres, it would be much easier, cheaper and safer to do it here on Earth.

IN THE SHADE

Rather than sending humans into space, we could try a sunshade. Placed between the Sun and the Earth, a vast reflective device could divert a proportion of sunlight (and therefore heat) before it reaches us. Sending a ginormous parasol into space would be too difficult, but a more practical solution could be to launch trillions of mini-spacecraft a million miles above Earth, forming a cloud around 100,000 kilometres long. Each of the devices would be made of a transparent film that could deflect light in different directions and weigh no more than a butterfly. Still, it would take at least ten years to get them all into orbit and cost a few trillion pounds. In reality, this might be better spent fixing things down here on the ground!

WHAT CAN I DO?

The future doesn't have to be the worst-case scenario. It could be the best! There are loads of ideas in this book that scientists and engineers are working on, but what can you do to help? Here are a few things you can do to get the eco-ball rolling, and begin making the world a cleaner, greener place. Make sure to ask an adult to help with any of these before trying them out.

Start your own wormery. Get a large plastic box, put holes in the bottom (adults can help with this), line it with newspaper or cardboard so your worms don't fall out and put it on bricks so air can get into the holes. Place a tray underneath (to catch any goop that falls out) and fill the box with soil and worms! You can feed your worms kitchen scraps instead of binning them.

Try going plastic-free for a week! Next time your parents are food shopping, go with them and see if you can spot items that don't come in plastic packaging.

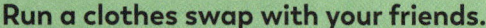

Run a clothes swap with your friends. Suggest everyone brings along their old T-shirts, jeans and jumpers then swap them with each other. New clothes that haven't cost the Earth!

Recycle rainwater. Collect it in buckets and use it to water your garden or houseplants, rather than turning on the tap.

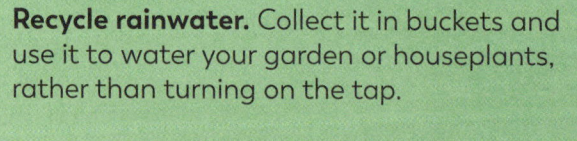

Try out some insect snacks. Rather than going out into the garden to forage for slugs, ask an adult to help you find far more delicious salt-and-pepper locusts or chocolate-covered crickets online or at specialist shops.

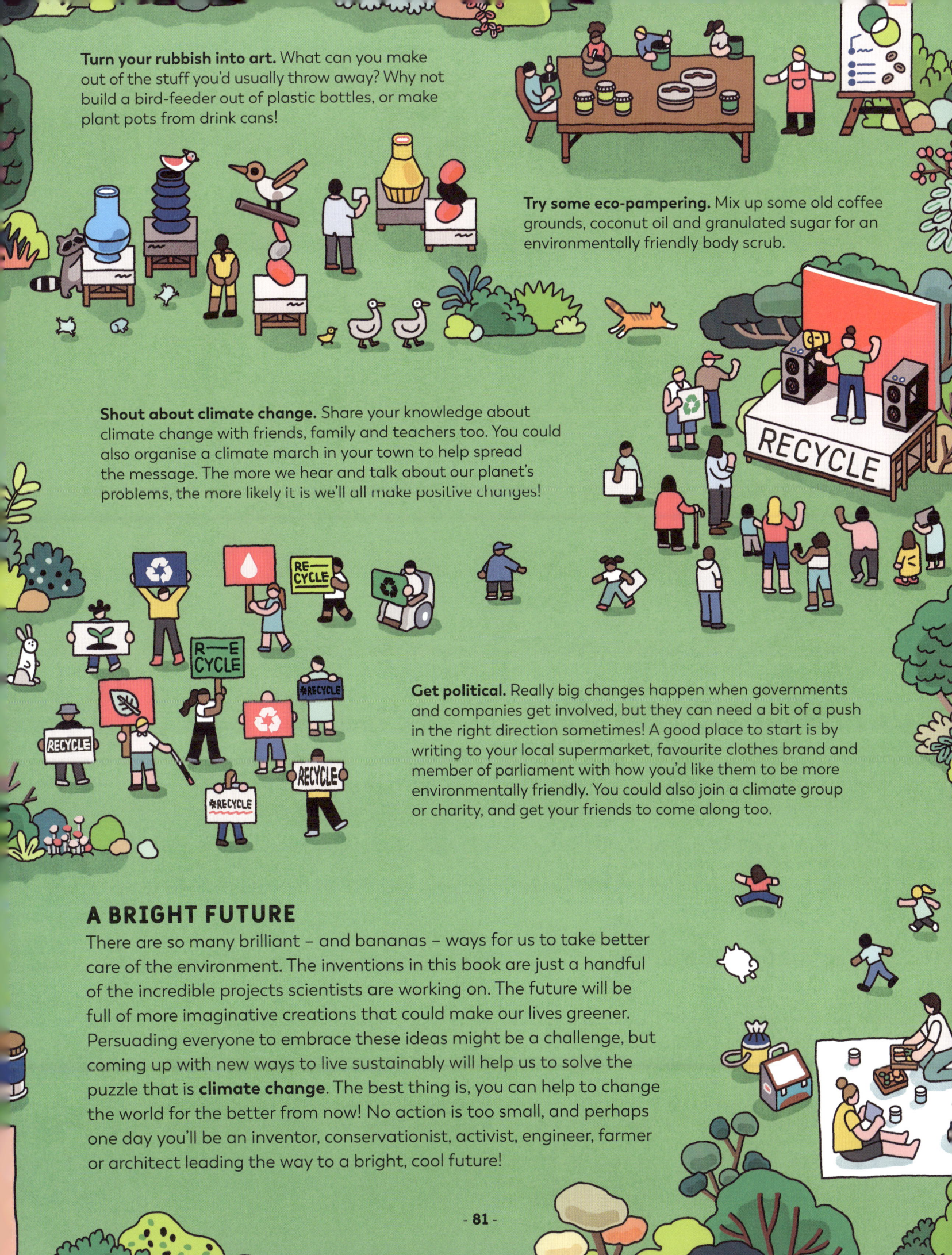

Turn your rubbish into art. What can you make out of the stuff you'd usually throw away? Why not build a bird-feeder out of plastic bottles, or make plant pots from drink cans!

Try some eco-pampering. Mix up some old coffee grounds, coconut oil and granulated sugar for an environmentally friendly body scrub.

Shout about climate change. Share your knowledge about climate change with friends, family and teachers too. You could also organise a climate march in your town to help spread the message. The more we hear and talk about our planet's problems, the more likely it is we'll all make positive changes!

Get political. Really big changes happen when governments and companies get involved, but they can need a bit of a push in the right direction sometimes! A good place to start is by writing to your local supermarket, favourite clothes brand and member of parliament with how you'd like them to be more environmentally friendly. You could also join a climate group or charity, and get your friends to come along too.

A BRIGHT FUTURE

There are so many brilliant – and bananas – ways for us to take better care of the environment. The inventions in this book are just a handful of the incredible projects scientists are working on. The future will be full of more imaginative creations that could make our lives greener. Persuading everyone to embrace these ideas might be a challenge, but coming up with new ways to live sustainably will help us to solve the puzzle that is **climate change**. The best thing is, you can help to change the world for the better from now! No action is too small, and perhaps one day you'll be an inventor, conservationist, activist, engineer, farmer or architect leading the way to a bright, cool future!

GLOSSARY

AI (ARTIFICIAL INTELLIGENCE) Machines have artificial intelligence when they can do things that usually require human intelligence, like solving difficult problems on their own.

AIR POLLUTION Substances in the air that are bad for the health of living things.

ALGAE A large and diverse range of organisms, from pond scum to giant kelp, that make their own fuel using photosynthesis. Unlike plants, algae don't have roots, stems or leaves, and many of them live in watery environments.

ALGORITHM A set of step-by-step instructions for solving a problem or performing an action, usually by a computer.

ATMOSPHERE The gases that surround a planet, held in place by gravity.

ATOM The building blocks of all matter in our universe, made of three parts – protons and neutrons which cluster together in a central nucleus, and electrons which orbit the nucleus.

AUGMENTED REALITY Technology that adds extra information, like words, pictures or sounds, on top of a real-world experience.

BACTERIA Microscopic living things made from a single cell that can be found almost everywhere on Earth.

BIODEGRADABLE Can be decomposed by microorganisms, like bacteria.

BIODIGESTER A device in which millions of bacteria break down food, animal and human waste, producing a mixture of gases like methane and carbon dioxide that can be used as a fuel source.

BIODIVERSITY The range and variety of life on our planet.

BIOMIMICRY Learning from and mimicking nature to solve human challenges.

BIOPSY Taking a sample of cells or tissue from a living thing.

CARBON DIOXIDE A greenhouse gas made from one carbon atom joined to two oxygen atoms, known as CO_2 – the 'C' stands for carbon, the 'O' for oxygen, and the '2' tells us that there are two oxygen atoms.

CARBON FOOTPRINT The amount of carbon dioxide that ends up in the atmosphere because of a person or activity.

CENTRIFUGE A machine that can spin objects inside it really fast.

CORAL BLEACHING A process that occurs when coral reefs expel the colourful, microscopic algae inside them, causing the coral to turn white.

CLIMATE CHANGE Long-term changes to the global temperature, environment and weather patterns.

CROSS-BREEDING Mixing different types of plants or animals to create an offspring with particular traits, like bigger leaves or fluffier fur.

DNA A material found in cells that contains the instructions a living thing needs to grow and function.

DRONE An aircraft without human pilots onboard.

ECOSYSTEMS The interaction between a collection of living things and their environment.

ELECTRIC CARS Cars powered by electricity rather than fuels like petrol or diesel.

ENERGY The ability to change or move. Energy can be converted from one form to another, but can never be created or destroyed.

EVAPORATION The process through which a liquid turns into a gas.

EXTINCTION When the last of a kind of plant or animal dies out.

FOSSIL FUELS Non-renewable fuels, dug up from the ground, that formed over millions of years from decomposing plants and organisms like algae and plankton. The three main fossil fuels are coal, oil and natural gas.

FUNGI Living things, including mushrooms, moulds and yeasts, that absorb food from what's around them and can range in size from microscopic to many metres.

GENES Sections of DNA that encode our individual characteristics, like hair or eye colour.

GLOBAL WARMING The heating of Earth's atmosphere caused by greenhouse gases.

GRAVITY A force by which things with mass (like apples, humans and planets) attract other things with mass. The reason we don't float into space is because we are drawn to the Earth's centre by the force of gravity.

GREENHOUSE GASES Gases in the atmosphere that trap heat coming in from the Sun or leaving Earth's surface, acting like a greenhouse.

HEAT PUMP A device that can move heat from one place to another.

HELIUM A gas lighter than the air around us, used to fill balloons.

HOLOGRAM A three-dimensional image made using light.

HYDROGEN The most abundant element in the universe. On Earth, hydrogen is a colourless but very flammable gas.

INFRARED Radiation with longer wavelengths than visible light, which we can't see (without special goggles) but can feel as heat.

INTERNATIONAL SPACE STATION (ISS) A large spacecraft that is orbiting around the Earth, used to perform science experiments.

LARVAE A stage many animals go through after hatching or birth, before transforming into an adult. Caterpillars are the larval stage of butterflies and moths, for example.

METHANE A particularly potent greenhouse gas made from one carbon atom joined to two hydrogen atoms.

MICROORGANISMS Living things that are so small they can only be seen under a microscope.

MICROPLASTICS Pieces of plastic that are smaller than five millimetres in length.

MYCELIUM Part of a fungus that is made up of a network of thread-like strands, which mushrooms can sprout from.

NUCLEAR FUSION A reaction where two or more nuclei are forced together. This produces a bigger nucleus and releases energy.

NUCLEUS/NUCLEI The central part of an atom made up of protons and neutrons.

OXYGEN The gas we breathe, which makes up 21% of the atmosphere.

PERMAFROST Ground that stays totally frozen for at least two years, typically near the Earth's North and South Poles.

PHYTOPLANKTON Microscopic, aquatic organisms that photosynthesise to produce energy.

PIEZOELECTRIC MATERIALS Materials which produce an electric charge when pressed, squeezed or stretched.

POLLINATION The process by which pollen is moved from a male part to a female part of a plant, or between plants, allowing the plant to produce seeds.

SMOG Air which has been heavily polluted by things like smoke or emissions from vehicle exhausts.

SOLAR PANELS Devices used to absorb sunlight and convert it into electricity.

TORNADO A rapidly spinning column of air, reaching from the ground to a storm cloud above.

ULTRAVIOLET (UV) Radiation with shorter wavelengths than visible light, also present in sunlight. Most humans can't see UV, but it can burn our skin which is why we often need to wear sun cream.

WAVELENGTH The distance between peaks or troughs of waves. Radiation, like UV and infrared, travels in waves and carries energy. The shorter the wavelengths, the more energy is being carried.

WIND TURBINE A tower with blades attached to the top that rotate in wind and produce energy.

INDEX